PEOPLE AND HOMES

About this book

This book is about people who live in other countries—their houses and homes, clothes and food and their customs, languages and beliefs. You can read about people who live in steamy hot jungles, or freezing arctic lands, and find out what it is like to live in an African village or a Bedouin tent in the desert. A beautifully detailed picture chart shows how mud, stone, bricks, wood and other materials are used for building houses in different countries.

The book also tells you about peoples' crafts, folk dances and music. You can find out about festivals in India, China, Russia and Japan and see how people in other countries celebrate Christmas. The main world religions, including Judaism, Islam, Christianity and Hinduism are simply explained and you can read about tribal religions too.

Written and researched by
Carol Bowyer and Roma Trundle

Illustrated by
Bob Hersey, Rob McCaig and
Joseph McEwan

Designed by
Graham Round

Edited by
Jenny Tyler and Lisa Watts

Consultant editors:
Barry Dufour, Fellow of the Royal Anthropological Institute,
London, England and Lecturer in Education, School of
Education, University of Leicester, England.
Dr Peter Loizos, Lecturer in Social Anthropology at London
School of Economics, University of London, England.

Research assistant: Jane Chisholm
Additional designs by Anna Barnard

PEOPLE AND HOMES

Contents

Peoples of the world

Houses round the world

Peoples and their countries

There are over 150 countries in the world. Some of them are huge, with hundreds of millions of people, while others are as small as cities with populations of only a few thousand.

People in different countries have their own customs, traditions, languages and beliefs. Some of the large countries have lots of different peoples, each with their own customs and languages.

1 What is a country?

Each country has its government which rules the people. This picture shows Capitol Hill in Washington, U.S.A. where the American Government, called the Congress, meets.

2

Every country has a flag and most have a national anthem. The Union Jack, seen here on the Tower of London, is the flag of the United Kingdom.

3

Countries have their own money and stamps which can usually be used only within their boundaries. Coins, notes and stamps often have pictures of famous people or places on them.

4

People in different countries usually speak different languages. In some countries, several languages are spoken and used on signposts like this one in the Sahara Desert in Mali.

5

In Japan, it is a custom for people to greet each other by bowing. People in other countries have their own special customs too, such as shaking hands.

Travelling abroad

To travel to another country you need a travel document called a passport. This shows your nationality, and the country you come from.

You need special permission to enter some countries. In these cases, you must have a visa stamped in your passport by the country's embassy.

At the boundaries between countries there are barriers across the roads. Here the frontier police examine your passport and watch out for smugglers.

Before you can buy anything in another country, you have to get your money changed at a bank or *bureau de change*.

Flags

The red maple tree leaf on the Canadian flag is the symbol of Canada. This flag was first used in 1965.

The Union Jack, flag of the United Kingdom, is a combination of the red cross of St George, white cross of St Andrew and red cross of St Patrick.

The Australian flag shows the Southern Cross, a group of stars which can be seen in the Australian sky.

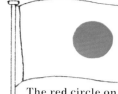

The red circle on the Japanese flag represents the sun and the name Japan means "land of the rising sun" in Japanese.

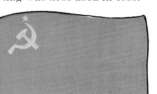

The hammer of the factory worker and the sickle of the farm worker appear on the flag of the U.S.S.R., which was first used in 1917.

The flag of the U.S.A. has 50 stars, one for each of the states. The 13 stripes represent the 13 original states.

On the flag of Saudi Arabia are the words "There is no god but God and Muhammad is his Prophet", written in Arabic.

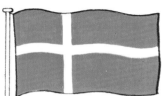

The Danish flag is the oldest in the world. It has been used for over 600 years.

Tribal peoples

In some parts of the world there are groups, or tribes of people whose customs and traditions are different from those of the country they live in. These peoples often have their own leaders, but they still have to obey the laws of the country they live in. Nowadays many of these people are moving to live in towns and are giving up their traditional ways of life.

The Bedouin are a people who live by herding camels and sheep in the Arabian desert. Nowadays, many of them are settling to live in the towns.

The Masai live in Kenya and Tanzania, in East Africa. They have their own language and live mainly by herding cattle.

Many different tribal peoples live in the Xingu National Park, a reservation in the Amazon forest, in South America.

Rich and poor countries

The rich countries are those which have lots of factories or large quantities of a natural product such as oil. Countries where most people work in factories or offices are called industrialized countries.

In the poorer countries most people still work on the land as farmers. They do not have many factories and often grow crops such as sugar, coffee or cotton to sell to the rich countries.

Country collections

There are lots of ways of making a country collection. You could collect everything you can find about one country, such as fruit and food wrappers, coins, stamps, postcards and pictures from travel brochures. Or you could limit your collection to one topic, such as stamps, or pictures of national costumes, flags or football players and collect these for lots of different countries.

Peoples' ancestors

Many millions of years ago, our ancestors were monkey-like creatures living in the trees. Like all other animals, people have slowly developed and changed to become as they are today.

Everyone in the world belongs to the same biological group, or species. This group is called *Homo sapiens*, which is Latin for "wise man".

These monkey-like creatures lived about 14 million years ago and are the ancestors of people. There were no people on Earth then.

The first people lived about three million years ago. They ate grubs and berries and hunted for animals which they killed with rocks and sticks.

Gradually, our early ancestors learned how to hunt larger animals. They made tools for cutting meat by chipping stones to give them sharp edges.

Tent made of animal skins.

For hundreds of thousands of years, people lived by hunting animals and collecting fruits to eat. There were no towns or villages and they lived in caves, or in huts built from sticks and animal skins or grass.

Chipping a rock to make a stone tool.

They were skilled at making sharp tools from stones, or from the bones or antlers of animals. They had not yet discovered how to weave cloth or to sew and their clothes were made from animal skins.

People first discovered they could grow food by planting seeds about 11,000 years ago. They settled near their farmland and built villages.

The villages gradually grew into towns. People learned how to weave and make pottery and trade things they made with people from other town

...aces of people

...ere are four main races of ...ople living in the world ...day, though all of them ...long to the same group, or ...ecies of mankind: *Homo ...piens.*

...Each race has its own special ...aracteristics, such as the ...rrow eyes of the Mongoloid ...ce, or the black skin of ...egroes. Scientists think that ...rly people in different parts ...the world gradually ...veloped characteristics that ...lped them to survive.

This Chinese boy belongs to the Mongoloid race.

Aboriginal boy from Australia belongs to the Australoid race.

This man from South Africa belongs to the Negroid race.

This Swiss girl belongs to the Caucasoid race.

Black skin protects people from the sun in very hot, wet places and the narrow eyes of Mongoloid people are a protection against extreme cold. Today racial differences are less important, because clothes, houses, heating and prepared foods enable people of any race to survive almost anywhere.

Tools

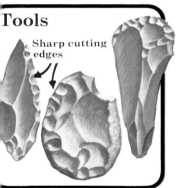

Sharp cutting edges

...eople first learned how ...make stone tools about ...million years ago. ...ter as they became ...ore skilful they made ...arp stone scrapers and ...ives.

Metals

Blowing on fire to make it hotter.

Metal tools were first made over 5,000 years ago. They lasted longer and were easier to make than stone tools. Copper and gold were used first.

Cooking

Cooking was probably learned by accident when meat fell into the fire. It made it tastier and easier to chew. People roasted food on hot stones.

Clothes

Bone needles were invented 40,000 years ago. They were used for sewing skins together with leather strips, and for decorating them with shells and teeth.

Beliefs

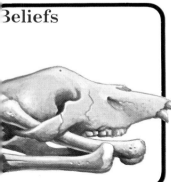

...is cave bear's skull ...th a leg bone through ...was found in a cave ...ere early people lived. ...ey probably believed it ...uld make magic.

Painting

People discovered how to paint with powdered coloured rocks, mixed with animal fat. Their brushes were made of animal hair.

Pottery

The Stone Age farmers were the first people to discover how to make pottery by baking clay in a fire. They made pots from coils of clay.

Writing

The marks on this piece of clay are some of the first writing. It was done by people called the Sumerians who lived about 5,000 years ago.

Language and writing

Over 4,000 languages are spoken in the world today. In some countries there are several languages and in India there are over 800. Sometimes people in one country speak different versions, or dialects of the same language. Some languages, such as English and Spanish, are spoken in many different parts of the world*

Here are six children from different countries speaking in their own languages.

Hej, jag heter, Margareta.

This is Swedish. It is pronounced "Hay, yag heer-ta Mar-gar-ret-a" and means "Hello, my name is Margareta".

Hola, me llamo Pablo.

This is Spanish. It is pronounced "O-la, may ya-mo Pablo" and means "Hello, my name is Pablo".

ЗДРАВСТВУЙТЕ МЕНЯ ЗОВУТ САША

This is Russian. It is pronounced "Is-drast-vooey-ti-ey men-yah zov-wot Sarsha" and means "Hello, my name is Sarsha"

Language families

People who study languages have discovered that many of them are related and can be grouped together into language families. This chart shows some of the languages in the Indo-European family. There are eight main groups in this language family. Two of the groups: Germanic and Romance, and some of the languages in them, are shown here.

INDO-EUROPEAN LANGUAGE FAMILY			
About half the world's peoples speak a language from this family.	**GERMANIC** The languages in this group developed from a language spoken long ago.	GERMAN	GUTEN MORGEN
		ENGLISH	GOOD MORNING
		DUTCH	GOEDE MORGEN
		SWEDISH	GOD MORGON
		NORWEGIAN	GOD MORGEN
	ROMANCE The languages in this group all developed from Latin. The words shown here mean "man" in English.	ITALIAN	UOMO
		SPANISH	HOMBRE
		FRENCH	HOMME
		PORTUGUESE	HOMEM
		ROMANIAN	OM

Writing

An alphabet is a set of symbols which stand for the sounds which make words. There are many different alphabets and ways of writing. Arabic is written from right to left, and Chinese does not have an alphabet at all. Instead it uses "characters" to stand for words or parts of words.

1 Latin or Roman alphabet

A B C D E
F G H I J K
L M N O P
Q R S T U
V W X Y Z

Most West European languages use this alphabet. Some of them add signs to the letters, e.g. ö, to show how they should be pronounced.

2 Arabic alphabet

ب ت ث ج ح
خ د ذ ر ز س
ش ص ض ط ظ
ع غ ف ق ك ل
م ن ھ و ي

3

	Picture signs	Modern Chinese character
Man		
Tree		
Bird		

All the languages in a family developed from the same parent language. As groups of people spread out across the world, they took their language with them. They began to pronounce words in a slightly different way from their ancestors, and had to find new words for foreign things, so gradually their language changed.

Arabic is the second most widely used alphabet. Other languages such as Persian and Urdu (used in Pakistan) are also written in it.

Modern Chinese characters developed from picture signs. The are now written from le to right, but used to be written in columns dow the page.

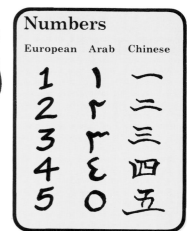

Numbers

European	Arab	Chinese
1	١	一
2	٢	二
3	٣	三
4	٤	四
5	٥	五

This is Arabic. It is pronounced "Mar-huba, ss-mee Layla" and means "Hello, my name is Layla".

This is Hindi which is spoken in India. It is pronounced "Nam-as-tay, mera naam Rah-day Shaam hi" and means "Hello, my name is Rahday Shaam".

This is Chinese. It is pronounced "Nee how, wah ming tzer Tsee-ow Hoong" and means "Hello, my name is Tseeow Hoong".

The numbers used in western Europe are called Arabic numerals and developed from numbers used by the Arabs 1,000 years ago. Chinese and some other languages have their own signs for numbers.

Greek

Greek was the first European language to have a written form. The word "alphabet" comes from the names of the first two Greek letters: *alpha* and *beta*.

African languages

This man is reading a newspaper written in Swahili, the main East African language. Over 1,000 languages are spoken in Africa. Some have no written form.

India

Hindi, which this girl is learning to read, is one of the languages of India. Many Indians speak Hindustani, a mixture of Hindi and another language called Urdu.

South America

PORTUGUESE
SPANISH
AMERICAN INDIAN

Many South American countries used to be ruled by Spain or Portugal, so Spanish and Portuguese are spoken there. American Indian languages are also spoken.

Arabic

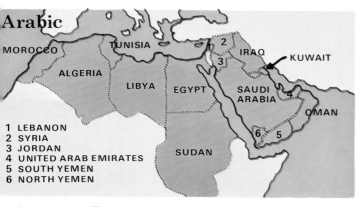

MOROCCO
TUNISIA
ALGERIA
LIBYA
EGYPT
IRAQ
KUWAIT
SAUDI ARABIA
OMAN
SUDAN

1 LEBANON
2 SYRIA
3 JORDAN
4 UNITED ARAB EMIRATES
5 SOUTH YEMEN
6 NORTH YEMEN

Arabic is the official language of all these countries. It spread out across these areas long ago, when followers of the Prophet Muhammad converted the people to their religion, Islam. The Islamic holy book, the Koran, is written in Arabic.

Chinese

There are lots of Chinese dialects, but everyone can understand these posters as they all use the same written language. The main dialect is Mandarin.

Written Chinese has over 40,000 different characters. Children at school need learn only about 3,000 of them for everyday use.

Money

Each country has its own money called its currency.*Some have the same name for their currency—more than 20 countries use "dollars"—but they all have different values.

The foreign exchange rate decides how much of another country's currency you can buy with your money. This rate often varies from day to day.

Notes and coins

Indian 100 rupee note. Writing is in eight Indian languages and English.

Greek 50 drachma note which shows the head of Helen of Troy, daughter of an ancient Greek god.

2 drachma piece

Spanish 100 peseta note with picture of a Spanish composer.

Iranian 50 rial note and 5 and 10 rial coins. Note shows ancient temple of Shiraz and antelope, old symbol of Iran.

1 Shops and shopping

This is a market called a *souk* in Jerusalem. There are no fixed prices and the stallkeeper and shopper argue about how much the goods are worth until they can agree a price.

2

In shops like this French greengrocer's the prices are fixed and shoppers do not usually bargain for a lower price.

4

This is an open-air market in Peru. Women bring food they have grown, but do not need to sell to other villagers.

*The chart on pages 92-95 shows what each country's currency is.

Japanese 1,000 yen note with picture of the Bank of Tokyo. Five yen coin with hole in it.

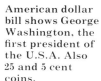
Malaysian sens. Picture on coin shows parliament building in Kuala Lumpur and Muslim crescent.

austrian 50 chilling note and schilling piece, hich shows old austrian head-ress.

Russian 5 rouble note showing one of the towers of the Kremlin, the government building.

American dollar bill shows George Washington, the first president of the U.S.A. Also 25 and 5 cent coins.

Australian 20 cent piece with picture of duck-billed platypus. One cent piece shows a possum.

Money collection

Sometimes, you find foreign money in your change, or you can ask people travelling abroad to save you some. You can also buy coins from dealers.

You could collect coins which have pictures of ships, animals or famous people, or according to the country they come from.

You could also make a collection of your own country's money, looking out for old or unusual coins.

3

Most big cities in the world have supermarkets which sell tinned and packaged foods. In America they stay open late nearly every night.

Living without money

Bushmen, who live in the Kalahari desert in Africa, use very little money. They hunt animals for food, build their own houses and make clothes from animal skins. Some are now beginning to work on farms for wages.

These people live and work on an Israeli kibbutz. They are given food and houses, and a little money for luxuries.

5

These women in a village in Iran are swopping a sack of grain for a carpet they have woven. Exchanging things like this is called bartering.

Money changers

This shopkeeper in Oman earns his living by buying and selling foreign currencies to tradesmen and travellers.

Storing wealth

The heavy gold earrings worn by this young Fulani girl from Africa, are her family's wealth. If they need money, they will sell some of the gold.

Unusual money

In this desert market in Ethiopia, people are paying for the things they need with bars of salt, which they use like money.

Food and cooking

In many countries, people eat very little meat. They have one main kind of filling food and eat it with sauces made with vegetables, spices or herbs. In Asia and the Middle East, the filling food is rice, in Africa it is maize, millet or white vegetables called yams. Potatoes are eaten in Europe and also in South America where they first came from. Everywhere people use flour made from wheat or other kinds of grain to make bread.

China

This family is eating steamed rice or noodles with vegetables and eggs or fish. Sometimes they flavour it with soya bean sauce. The Chinese do not eat much meat.

India

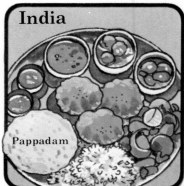

Pappadam

This is a special meal from western India. In the little bowls are rice, lentils, vegetable curry and crisps called pappadams. The curry is spicy but not always hot.

West Africa

Kitchen where food is cooked over a fire.

Millet

Forbidden foods

Some people do not eat certain foods because their religions forbid them. Hindus will not eat beef as cows are thought to be sacred and some do not eat any meat, fish or eggs as they are not supposed to kill animals. Muslims think pigs are unclean and do not eat pork. Jews have many rules and the foods which they may eat are called "kosher" foods.

Italy

This is a spaghetti-making machine. Spaghetti is a type of pasta made from wheat flour. It is cooked in different ways with meat, tomatoes, cheese or fish.

Germany

Many different kinds of sausages and smoked meats are eaten with warm, filling soups, pickled vegetables and rye bread called pumpernickel.

Cooking

In many parts of the world, outside the cities, people do not have gas or electric stoves. They cook over open fires or in clay ovens.

Cooking makes some foods tastier and easier to chew and digest. It also kills germs in the food. Cooked food usually keeps longer without going bad.

1 Before she can start cooking, this Indian woman has to light a wood fire. She cooks the food in shallow metal pans over the fire.

2 Women in a village in Cyprus share this clay oven for baking bread and pies. Most have stoves at home, but no ovens.

3 People who live in tents often barbeque their food on sticks. They have few pans to pack when they move camp.

Tall tower called a granary where grain is stored to keep it dry and away from rats.

women work with their babies strapped to their backs.

Bowl made from dried skin of a fruit called a gourd.

In many African countries people grow a grain called millet. These village women from Upper Volta are pounding it to make a coarse flour.

They make a kind of porridge from the millet flour and eat it with vegetables and a peppery sauce. Meat is eaten only on special occasions.

Tunisia

This Tunisian family are eating a bowl of cous-cous. This is coarsely ground wheat, boiled and eaten with a vegetable or meat sauce.

Peru

This woman is making special pancakes, called tortillas, and filling them with potato spiced with hot peppers and lemon for her family's lunch.

Milk and cheese

1

This is a dairy in Denmark. Huge herds of cows are milked quickly by machines to supply city people with milk.

2

People use the milk of lots of different animals such as sheep, goats, llamas and camels. This woman is milking a yak.

3

Milk keeps much longer if it is made into butter, cheese or yoghurt. This Bedouin woman is making butter in a goatskin.

4

These Swiss cheese makers are draining the "whey" from the solid milk "curds" which will be put in a mould to make a cheese called Emmental.

Gruyère from Switzerland — Brie from France — Manchego from Spain

Feta from Greece — Edam from Holland — Stilton from England

These are some cheeses from countries in Europe.

The hungry world

Half the people in the world do not have enough to eat and millions die every year from starvation. Floods and droughts, poverty and wars prevent people in the developing countries from getting enough to eat. In richer countries people suffer diseases caused by eating too much rich or processed food.

Recipe for an Indian drink

To make this Indian drink, called *lassi*, you need a pot of plain yogurt, cold water, sugar, vanilla essence and a screw-topped container.

Put the yogurt into the container, then fill the yogurt pot with cold water and pour it in too. Add a teaspoonful of sugar and about 3 drops of vanilla essence. Screw on the top of the container and shake the mixture well. It tastes best chilled or with ice.

To make strawberry *lassi*, use strawberry flavoured yogurt and leave out the sugar and vanilla. You could use other flavours of yogurt too.

Clothes

Traditional clothes are still worn in many parts of the world. These clothes are suited to the climate and do not change with fashion. Loose, flowing clothes, such as saris and sarongs, are cool to wear. Thick layers of fur or padded felt clothes help keep people warm. It is usually the women who still dress in the traditional way. Men and young people, especially in cities, are now buying western-styled clothes.

1 Clothes for hot countries

Saris, which are worn by Indian women, are 6m lengths of silk or cotton cloth. Under their saris, they wear petticoats and short blouses.

2

Men and women in South-East Asia wear sarongs. These are lengths of cotton cloth which they wrap round their waists and wear with shirts or embroidered blouses

Cold weather clothes

High in the Himalayan mountains, where the winters are bitterly cold, peoples' clothes are large and loose so they can wear lots of layers underneath. They are made of fur or thick felt and are often padded for extra warmth. The long, wide sleeves roll down to cover their hands, and ear-flaps protect their ears.

Hats and head-dresses

The light, straw, cone-shaped hats worn in South-East Asia, protect people from the sun and rain but are cool to wear.

A turban, like this man from Afghanistan is wearing, is a long piece of cloth wrapped round and round the head.

Arab men's head-dresses are plain white or have red or black patterns. The cloth is held on with a thick cord.

Village women in Boliv wear felt bowler hats. These were first worn years ago and were copied from Europeans

3 People who live in deserts wear thin loose clothes to keep cool. This Tuareg tribesman from the Sahara covers his face and head too, for protection against the burning sun and blowing sand.

4 Women in many African countries wear brightly coloured cloths which they wrap round themselves. Some women wear western-style dresses made from this material.

5 Some of the tribal peoples who live in hot, rainy jungles wear only waistbands. They often rub coloured plant juices on to their skins to keep off insects.

1 ## Special clothes

In some Muslim countries women have to cover themselves from head to foot before going out. These Arab women from the Yemen wear long black robes and face masks.

2 Policemen, like this French *gendarme*, **and** soldiers, nurses and people in many other jobs, wear special uniforms so that they can be recognized.

3 The coloured head-dresses of these Kirghiz women from Russia have special meanings. Married women wear red and unmarried girls wear white.

4 The cross-stitch embroidery on this Arab woman's dress shows which town she comes from. Women from different towns have different embroidery.

Fashion

Elderly Japanese women still wear their traditional kimonos but younger girls wear modern fashion clothes. Fashion trends are much the same all over the world.

National costume

Sporran

Tartan kilt

This Scotsman is wearing his national costume. Most European countries have national costumes but they are worn only on special occasions or for tourists.

Ideas for dressing up

SARONG
1. SHEET OR MATERIAL ABOUT 2m LONG SEW OR SAFETY PIN EDGES
2. FOLD ACROSS STOMACH AND TUCK IN AT WAIST HOLD HERE
3. FOLD OTHER SIDE OVER SAFETY PIN

SARI
1. LONG BIT OF MATERIAL eg. OLD SHEET TORN IN HALF LENGTH WAYS WITH ENDS SEWN TOGETHER TUCK EDGE INTO PANTS
2. BRING MATERIAL IN FRONT OF YOU AND FOLD TO MAKE 4 BIG PLEATS TUCK INTO PANTS
3. WIND MATERIAL BEHIND YOU, THEN
4. UP OVER YOUR LEFT SHOULDER

TURBAN
1. LONG SCARF OR BIT OF OLD SHEET
2. WIND ENDS ROUND FRONT OF HEAD
3. TUCK ENDS IN AT BACK

Hair, jewellery and make-up

People arrange their hair, paint their faces and wear jewellery to make themselves more attractive to others. People from different parts of the world have very different styles of decorating themselves. What some people think beautiful, others, with different traditions, may find very ugly. Women usually dress themselves up more than men, but among some tribal peoples, the men often spend hours decorating themselves.

Jewellery

The silver bands and coins worn by this woman from Laos are her family's savings and show how rich they are.

This Amazon jungle woman wears seeds and monkey's teeth. People often make jewellery from things they find.

Indian women sometimes wear rings in their noses. This shows that they are married.

Sometimes jewellery shows a person's religion. This Christian girl wears a cross.

Masai women, who live in East Africa, wear many necklaces made from coloured glass beads. Some bind their arms and legs with metal rings, and it is shameful for a married woman to be seen without her earrings.

Hair and hairstyles

People of different races have different types of hair. You can see the three main types below.

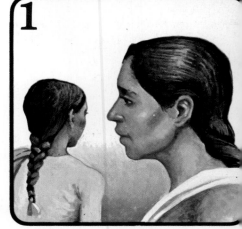

People of the Caucasoid race have straight or wavy hair. It may be blond, brown, reddish-brown or black.

Mongoloid people have thick, straight, black hair, and very little hair on their faces or bodies.

Negroes have dark, tightly curled hair. This probably developed as a protection against the hot sun.

In India, people think it is unfeminine for women to have short hair. They often wear it in long plaits. Young women are now breaking with this tradition and cutting their hair.

14

Make-up and body paint

Since prehistoric times people have painted and decorated their bodies. Over 5,000 years ago the Egyptians used eye make-up called kohl, made from a powdered rock. Kohl is still used in India and the Middle East.

Women all over the world use make-up. Modern make-up is made from chemical dyes and plant and animal oils.

This woman from the jungle in Peru paints her face with vegetable dyes. The patterns show which tribe she comes from.

At festival time, Huichol women from Mexico stick petals on their faces with lipstick so the gods know they want children.

Sailors learned how to tattoo from Pacific Islanders. The pattern is pricked into the skin and colour is rubbed in.

Since childhood, this woman from the Amazon jungle has worn little bits of wood stuck through her lips.

Hair plastered with beeswax and dusted with colour.

Mirror

Paint made from powdered rocks.

Men of the Nuba people, from Sudan, paint their bodies to make them look strong and healthy. They oil their skins and then colour them with powdered red or yellow rocks, black ashes or crushed white shells.

How to paint your face

Here are some Nuba face patterns you could try out. You can buy face paints at toy shops or theatre suppliers, or you could use old make-up. Use cold cream to remove your face paint.

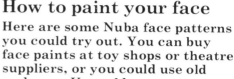
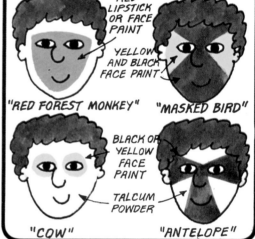

RED LIPSTICK OR FACE PAINT

YELLOW AND BLACK FACE PAINT

"RED FOREST MONKEY"   "MASKED BIRD"

BLACK OR YELLOW FACE PAINT

TALCUM POWDER

"COW"   "ANTELOPE"

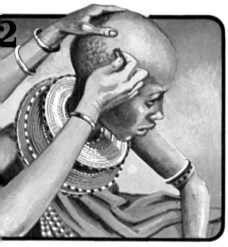

2

Masai women shave their heads to make themselves more beautiful and show off their colourful jewellery. They shave on special occasions with razor blades and a mixture of milk and water.

3

It is the Masai warriors who wear their hair long. They spend several days dressing each other's hair, coating it with a mixture of red soil called ochre and animal fat. They rub the strands together to make little twisted ropes of hair and gather them together with clips of wood. Masai men often put sweet-smelling leaves under their arms to make them smell nice. They, too, wear lots of jewellery.

Crafts

In many parts of the world people still make the things they need by hand. Some countries are famous for the work done by their craftsmen. Beautiful carpets are made in Iran, fine lace is made in Spain, Morocco is famous for its leather crafts and Indonesia for its silver work. Most craftsmen work with traditional tools and to patterns and designs that have been followed for hundreds of years. Nowadays they sell most of their work to tradesmen.

Weaving

Most cloth is now made in factories by machines, but some craftsmen still use hand looms to weave sheep's wool, goats' hair, cotton and silk into cloth.

1 Baskets

This English man is making a basket with willow sticks. Good baskets cannot be made by machines, so they are still made by hand all over the world.

Mexican women weave brightly coloured cotton cloth for clothes. Weaving is done on looms which hold the long "warp" threads tight while the coloured threads are woven in and out with wooden shuttles. This back-strap loom is easy to pack up and carry around.

Spinning

Cotton and wool must be spun into yarn before they can be woven. This Greek woman is spinning wool on a spindle.

2

Sticks, leaves, grasses and straw can all be woven to make baskets. This Kraho Indian woman from Brazil weaves baskets of palm leaves for carrying fruit.

Carpet making

In Turkey, carpets are made by knotting short pieces of wool on to the upright threads of wall looms. They are made by women and girls working at home. Carpets of different designs and colours are made in different regions.

Dyeing

The yarn is dyed with natural plant colours or chemical dyes. In Morocco, men dye wool in big pits or vats.

16

Pottery

Pottery is made from clay which is baked until it becomes hard. In many countries, local village potters make clay pots for the villagers to carry water or store food in.

Smooth, even pots are made by shaping the clay while it spins round on a wheel. This Turkish man works as a potter and sells his pots to shops in the towns.

Egyptian women buy huge pots from village potters to carry water from the well. Many of them do not have running water in their homes.

In this pueblo village in the state of New Mexico, U.S.A., an Indian woman is shaping a pot from coils of clay. She smooths the coils together with her fingers. When the pot has been baked, she will paint on it special patterns which have been used in this region for hundreds of years. Villagers and tourists buy the pots.

Batik

In Indonesia, patterns are made on cloth by a special method called *batik*. This woman is painting the pattern with melted wax from a wooden pen. When the cloth is dyed, the colour does not sink into the waxed areas. Later she paints more wax patterns and re-dyes the cloth to make beautiful and intricate patterns.

Carving

Dutch craftsmen still carve wooden clogs by hand. They sell them to tourists as few people in Holland now wear clogs.

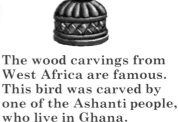

The wood carvings from West Africa are famous. This bird was carved by one of the Ashanti people, who live in Ghana.

How to paint wax pictures

You can use the batik method to paint unusual pictures.

1. DRAW PATTERN ON PAPER WITH WHITE CANDLE

3. WHEN DRY, DO SOME MORE WAX PATTERNS

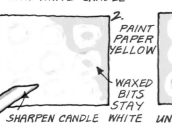

2. PAINT PAPER YELLOW

WAXED BITS STAY WHITE

SHARPEN CANDLE WITH SCISSORS

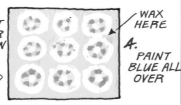

WAX HERE

4. PAINT BLUE ALL OVER

UNWAXED BITS GO GREEN (YELLOW + BLUE = GREEN)

Bark painting

Australian Aboriginals are well-known for the paintings they do on bark from eucalyptus trees. This is a painting of a kangaroo.

17

Beliefs

People round the world have different beliefs and belong to different religions. On pages 84–87, you can find out about the main world religions followed by people from many different countries.*

Tribal peoples have their own religions and beliefs. As they are giving up their traditional ways of life, however, they are also changing their beliefs. Many tribal peoples now belong to one of the world religions, such as Christianity or Islam.

These flute players in the Amazon jungle pray to their gods with music. They are asking them to end the rainy season so they can start fishing again.

This Aboriginal man from Australia is doing a wind dance. The rustle of the leaves tied to his legs makes a sound like the wind which he hopes will bring fish to the shore.

Frightening off spirits

The Ho people in eastern India believe in spirits which live in plants. This priest is thanking the spirit of the harvest for protecting the crop, by offering it a cock.

Villagers in Nigeria leave food for the spirits of their ancestors at this shrine. They believe the spirits will bring bad luck if they are not looked after.

Some Chinese, especially in Hong Kong, believe that their ancestral spirits protect them. In return they offer food and burn incense at their graves.

Witchcraft

In this street market in South Africa you can buy medicines to keep away witches. Many tribal peoples in Africa believe that illness and misfortune can be caused by witches' spells.

This man from the Ivory Coast is a witch-finder. He looks into a bowl of water and sees the faces of witches who have put spells on people.

The magic things in this Angolan man's bowl help him to find witches. He shakes them and reads answers in the way they fall.

Some witch-finders use rubbing boards like this. They ask questions and slide the knob along the board. When it sticks they know the answer.

18   *The chart on pages 28-31 shows the religions practised in each country.*

Mask to frighten spirits.

Mask to hide person

Mask that looks like a bird.

For special ceremonies and dances, tribal peoples often wear masks. Sometimes these are to hide them from evil spirits, or frighten off dangerous ghosts. Other masks are worn so that people can talk to spirits without being recognized.

By the light of a full moon, these Karaja Indians from Brazil dance through their village dressed in coconut fibre and grasses. They stamp their feet and shake rattles to frighten away evil spirits.

Ideas for making masks

Here are some ideas for making masks.

CARDBOARD MASK

1. CUT A PIECE OF CARD TO COVER YOUR FACE

EYE HOLES

STRING HOLES

MOUTH HOLE

2. PAINT AND DECORATE MASK

PAPER TONGUE GLUED ON TO MASK

FEATHERS OR LEAVES

DRINKING STRAW MASK

STRING HOLES

BEND 10cm FROM END

EYE HOLES

BEND

1. CUT A STRIP OF CARD 50cm LONG, 10cm WIDE

LONG STRAWS

STRING

CUT STRAWS TO FIT

2. STICK STRAWS ON WITH STICKY TAPE

Useful things for decorating masks: string, wool, raffia, paints, bottle tops, silver paper, feathers.

The evil eye

Some people believe that sickness and bad luck can be caused by people looking at them with the "evil eye". To protect themselves they wear charms. People round the world have different superstitions. In Britain, horseshoes are believed to bring good luck.

1

Blue beads, like those on the harness of this Greek bull, are supposed to ward off the evil eye. Silver charms shaped like hands are also supposed to give protection.

2

Fishermen in Portugal paint eyes on their boats. They are said to help them catch a lot of fish because the eyes can "see" where the fish are.

3

This Nuba girl from the Sudan, in Africa, wears special herbs in pouches round her neck. These keep away evil spirits and help to bring her good luck.

World religions

Judaism

Judaism is the religion of the Jewish people. There are about 12 million Jews. Over three million of them live in Israel, where Judaism began over 3,000 years ago.

Jews believe that there is one God and that they have a special duty to worship him. They believe that they are descended from a tribe of people called the Hebrews, and that God chose two of the Hebrew people, Abraham and Moses, to be his messengers.

Jews believe that God gave Moses the Ten Commandments, written on stone tablets. The Commandments are rules saying how people should live together and worship God.

This Rabbi, or Jewish teacher, is reading from the Jews' most holy book, called the Torah. The Torah is written by hand in the Hebrew language and Jews believe it contains God's words to Moses.

The Sabbath is a holy day for Jews. It begins on Friday at sunset, when Jewish families eat a special Sabbath meal and light the Sabbath candles. It ends when it gets dark on Saturday.

On the Sabbath Jews worship God in the synagogue. When boys are 13 and girls are 12 they should begin to live by the Jewish traditions. This is called the age of Bar-mitzvah.

This is the Western Wall in Jerusalem where Jews go to pray. It is the remains of an ancient temple which was destroyed over 2,000 years ago and is a very holy place for Jews.

Christianity

Christians believe that a man called Jesus Christ, born nearly 2,000 years ago, was the son of God.

When Jesus was born, some Jews believed he was the "Messiah", sent from God to bring peace on Earth. They became the first Christians. Followers of Jesus spread his teachings across the world and today, nearly a quarter of all the people in the world is Christian.

The life of Jesus is described in the New Testament, part of a book called the Bible which is holy to Christians. Jesus spent his life teaching about God and healing people. He chose 12 followers, or disciples, to be with him and carry on his work. Christians also believe, like Jews, that Abraham and Moses were messengers of God.

Islam

[Pe]ople who follow the religion [of] Islam are called Muslims. [T]hey believe there is one God [w]hom they call Allah, and that [th]e Prophet Muhammad, who [w]as born 1,400 years ago in [M]ecca, Arabia, was the [m]essenger of God. Muslims [be]lieve that Abraham, Moses [an]d Jesus were also God's [m]essengers. The followers of [M]uhammad spread the ideas of [Is]lam through the Middle East. [To]day it is the main religion of [al]l the Arab countries, and also [in] Pakistan and parts of Africa [an]d South-East Asia.

Minaret—the tall tower of a mosque.

Building called the Kaaba.

[T]he Muslim holy book is [ca]lled the Koran. Muslims [be]lieve the Koran is an [ac]count of God's words to [M]uhammad and it is [al]ways written in Arabic. [Th]is is a page from a very [ol]d Koran.

From the tall tower of a mosque, a man calls Muslims to prayer. They are supposed to pray five times a day. Before they go in to a mosque they should take off their shoes and wash.

If they are not near a mosque, Muslims can spread out prayer mats and say their prayers. They turn to face in the direction of the city of Mecca and recite from the Koran.

Mecca is a holy place for Muslims. Once in their lives, if they can, they are supposed to make a pilgrimage to the city. There, they pray at the holy building called the Kaaba.

2

3

4

[Je]sus died by being [cr]ucified, which means he [w]as nailed to a cross. In [hi]s lifetime he was loved [an]d followed by many [pe]ople, but some of the [Je]ws feared his power.

Christians believe that Jesus rose from the dead and now lives with God in heaven. They believe that if they lead good lives, they too will go to heaven when they die.

On Sundays, Christians go to church to worship God. This picture shows the church of the Holy Sepulchre in Jerusalem which traditionally marks the place where Jesus was buried.

When people become Christians they promise to try and follow Jesus and are baptized. Most Christians are baptized when they are babies and their godparents make the promise for them.

Hinduism

Hinduism began about 4,000 years ago and is the oldest world religion. There are about 500 million Hindus, most of whom live in India.

Hindus believe in reincarnation, that is, they believe that when people die, they are born again into other bodies until they are good enough to be united with God. If people lead bad lives, they believe they may be reborn as animals.

1

This is a statue of a Hindu god called Shiva, Lord of Dance. Hindus worship many gods and goddesses but they believe that each one represents a form of the highest God.

2

Hindus often have shrines in their homes, where they worship their gods. They pray and light candles at the shrines, make offerings of food and read stories about the gods from their holy books.

3

Temple

The River Ganges is a very sacred place for Hindus and they make pilgrimages to it. They wash away their sins in the water and float trays of flowers and incense on the river as offerings to the gods.

Buddhism

Buddhism was started in India about 2,500 years ago by a man called Gautama who is known as the Buddha. He taught that suffering is caused by people's selfish behaviour and that if they try to lead good lives they will be happy and have peace of mind. Buddhists believe that they are born again and again into this world, until they reach Nirvana, a state of everlasting peace.

This is a golden statue of Buddha in front of which Buddhists meditate about his teachings. He wanted to be thought of as a guide and not as an idol to be worshipped.

To help them lead better lives and move nearer to Nirvana, Buddhists visit shrines where they make offerings of food and flowers and meditate on Buddha's teachings.

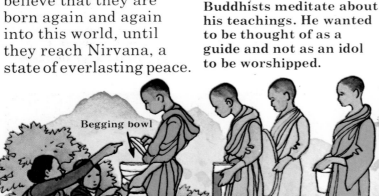

Begging bowl

Many Buddhist men live in monasteries for a few weeks and some spend their lives as monks. They shave their heads, wear yellow robes and carry begging bowls for food. They lead very simple lives and spend much time meditating. They also teach children about Buddhism and take care of funerals and other ceremonies. Buddhists believe that if they try and follow the example of the monks, it will help them reach Nirvana.

This wheel carved in stone is a Buddhist symbol. The eight spokes stand for the main points of Buddha's teachings.

When Hindus die their bodies are burned and the ashes are sprinkled in rivers. Their families pray that their souls will find their way to God and not be reborn again into this world.

The caste system

Every Hindu is born into a group called a caste. Some of the castes are thought to be higher and purer than others and priests come from the highest caste.

One of the most important Hindu duties is to obey caste rules. Different castes are supposed to do different work and they are not supposed to marry people from other castes.

Some people in India think the caste system is unfair and are trying to change it.

Hindus have great respect for animals because they believe that everything has a soul. Cows are specially sacred and are allowed to wander freely in the streets.

This man is a shoemaker and he is a member of one of the lowest castes, called the Harijans. Hindus believe that if they obey caste rules they may be reborn into higher castes.

Sikhism

This religion was begun by Guru Nanak, a spiritual leader who lived in India about 500 years ago. He taught that the caste system was wrong and that people should worship only one god. Today there are about 12 million Sikhs.

Sikhs worship God in their temples and read from the Granth, their holy book which contains the teachings of their leaders or "Gurus".

Sikh men and women are not supposed to cut their hair. The men wear turbans to keep it in place and silver bangles on their wrists.

Map of world religions

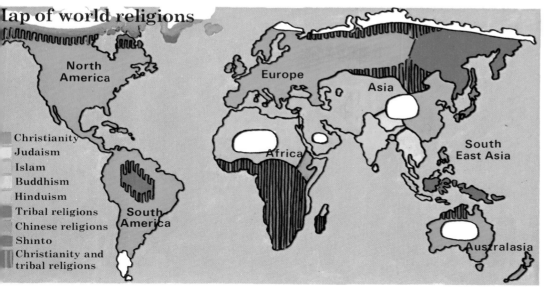

- Christianity
- Judaism
- Islam
- Buddhism
- Hinduism
- Tribal religions
- Chinese religions
- Shinto
- Christianity and tribal religions

Shinto

Shinto is an ancient religion which is practised in Japan. People worship spirits at shrines where they hang prayer notes and offer food and money.

Celebrations and festivals

All round the world, festivals are times when people dress up in their best clothes, eat special food and give presents.

In most countries, the main festivals celebrate special events in people's religions, such as the birth of a prophet. Other celebrations mark the coming of the new year, or special days such as birthdays.

Christmas

Every year on 25 December, Christians celebrate Christmas to remember the birth of Jesus Christ. Christians in different countries have their own special customs which take place during the Christmas season. Many have stories about St Nicholas, known as Santa Claus, who brings presents.

On 6 December, St Nicholas' Day, Santa Claus fills children's shoes with presents and takes the straw and carrots they leave for his horse.

Lady Befana brings gifts on 6 January. Legend say she was too busy to visit Jesus when he was born, so now she looks for him at every house.

People dress up in masks and straw to tease children. They pretend to be the companions of St Nicholas who used to punish naughty children.

Early in the morning on St Lucia's day, 13 December, young girls wearing crowns of candles offer people special wheat cakes.

Christmas decorations called pinatas are full of sweets and nuts. Children are blindfolded and have to try and break the pinatas with sticks.

This Burmese girl is lighting candles to honour Buddha's birthday. Buddhists also celebrate the day a man becomes a monk.

New Year

New Year is celebrated on different days around the world because people use different systems to work out their calendars. In some countries the New Year begins on a different day each year.

Many New Year customs probably began as ways of chasing away the evil spirits of the old year and welcoming good fortune.

In parts of India, the Hindu New Year is marked by the Diwali festival. Patterns of rice flour on doorsteps welcome the goddess of wealth.

Chinese people all over the world celebrate their New Year with dragon dances and firecrackers to frighten away evil spirits.

Hindu festivals

There are many festivals in India as Hindus have lots of gods to honour. This is the "Car" festival for the god Juggernaut*, Lord of the Universe. Huge carts with statues of the god, attended by priests, are pulled through the streets.

Weddings

At Greek weddings, after the church ceremony, it is the custom for guests to pin paper money on the bride and bridegroom.

Arab Muslim marriages usually take place at home. A marriage contract is signed and then there is a party for relatives and friends.

Jewish festivals

Jews celebrate many events believed to have happened in their history. The Passover festival reminds them of when Moses rescued their ancestors, the Israelites, from slavery over 3,000 years ago. The Israelites had to escape quickly and did not have time to let their bread rise. To remind them of this, Jews eat flat, unleavened bread, during Passover week.

For the Sukkot festival, people build little huts in their gardens. This reminds them of how their ancestors lived in the wilderness.

Muslim feast

During the month of Ramadan, Muslims are supposed to fast. They may not eat or drink during daylight hours. At the end of the month they feast and give presents.

In Hindu marriage ceremonies, the couple are joined with a white cloth. Parents usually choose whom their children should marry.

May Day

On 1 May, May Day, parades of soldiers and people with red flags march through Red Square, in Moscow, U.S.S.R. They are celebrating the achievements of the working people.

How to make a pinata

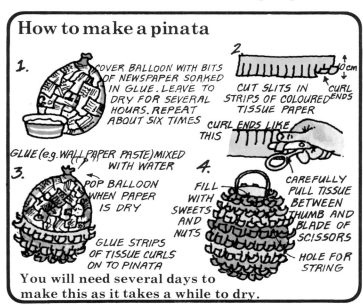

1. COVER BALLOON WITH BITS OF NEWSPAPER SOAKED IN GLUE. LEAVE TO DRY FOR SEVERAL HOURS. REPEAT ABOUT SIX TIMES

GLUE (e.g. WALLPAPER PASTE) MIXED WITH WATER

2. CUT SLITS IN STRIPS OF COLOURED TISSUE PAPER — CURL ENDS

CURL ENDS LIKE THIS

3. POP BALLOON WHEN PAPER IS DRY

GLUE STRIPS OF TISSUE CURLS ON TO PINATA

4. FILL WITH SWEETS AND NUTS — CAREFULLY PULL TISSUE BETWEEN THUMB AND BLADE OF SCISSORS

HOLE FOR STRING

You will need several days to make this as it takes a while to dry.

For Shinto weddings in Japan, the bride often wears a kimono and changes into modern clothes for the reception.

This is the origin of our word juggernaut, meaning large truck.

Music and dancing

In the past, people in Europe and America danced their traditional folk dances at fairs, festivals, weddings and celebrations. Folk dances are very old and the steps have been passed down from parents to children for hundreds of years. Nowadays they are mostly performed by dance groups in national costumes.

In other parts of the world, people have traditional dances which they perform at festivals or use to tell stories of their gods and heroes.

Balinese dancers

The flamenco dances of southern Spain are usually danced by gypsies to the music of guitars. They wear frilly skirts and make clicking sounds with castanets.

In Russian Cossack dancing, the men do somersaults and high kicks to show their skill. These dances were first done by Cossack soldiers several hundred years ago.

In India, Hindus worship their gods with dances. They use movements of their hands and eyes to tell stories about the gods.

On the island of Bali, in Indonesia, dancers act out stories about their Hindu gods with intricate movements of their eyes and bodies. Before the dances, which are often performed in temples, offerings of fruit and flowers are made to the gods. The dancers wear richly coloured silk costumes and head-dresses.

Balinese children begin to learn to dance when they are about six years old. It takes years of training to master the movements.

The dancers need perfect muscle control to perform the delicate hand and arm movements, all of which have special meanings.

This dancer is dressed up as the wicked witch, Rangda. Many of the dances are stories about the triumph of good over evil.

Musical instruments

Each region of the world has its own folk music which is played on traditional musical instruments to accompany folk dances.

The Spanish guitar probably developed from instruments like the Arabic "ud", shown on the right.

The Arabic ud is a kind of lute which is played by plucking the strings. It is used in classical and folk music.

The sitar is an Indian instrument which has six or seven strings. The person playing it sits on the floor and plucks the strings with their fingers.

Bagpipes are played to accompany Scottish sword dances. Air from the bag is forced through the pipes to make sounds.

In Indonesia, xylophones, gongs, bamboo pipes and drums are played in village orchestras.

Drums are often played in African music. Here they are being heated so that they make the right sounds.

4 Japanese Kabuki plays are a mixture of mime, music and dance. People offstage chant stories about ancient heroes and the actors wear traditional costume.

5 These Zulu men in South Africa are doing a warrior dance. In the past these were performed before battles, but now Zulus do them for tourists.

6 The Maori people of New Zealand dress up in their traditional clothes and dance on special occasions. Many of the dances tell stories of the Maoris' past.

Peoples of the world chart

PEOPLE	WHERE THEY LIVE	LANGUAGE	RELIGION	CURRENCY
Afghans	Afghanistan	Dari Persian, Pushtu	Muslim	Afghani (100 puls)
Albanians	Albania	Albanian	Muslim, Christian	Lek (100 qintars)
Algerians	Algeria	Arabic, Berber, French	Muslim	Dinar (100 centimes)
Americans	United States of America	English	Christian, Jewish	U.S. dollar (100 cents)
Andorrans	Andorra	Catalan, French, Spanish	Christian	French franc and Spanish peseta
Angolans	Angola	Portuguese, Bantu languages	Christian, tribal religions	Angolan escudo (100 centavos)
Arabs	Egypt, Syria, Jordan, Kuwait, United Arab Emirates, Oman, Saudi Arabia, Lebanon, Israel, Qatar, Bahrain, Libya, Tunisia, Algeria, Morocco, North and South Yemen	Arabic	Muslim	Money of countries where they live
Argentinians	Argentina	Spanish	Christian	Argentinian peso
Australians	Australia	English	Christian	Australian dollar (100 cents)
Austrians	Austria	German	Christian	Schilling (100 groschen)
Bahamians	Bahamas	English	Christian	Bahamian dollar
Bahrainis	Bahrain	Arabic	Muslim, Christian	Bahraini dinar
Bangladeshis	Bangladesh	Bengali	Muslim, Hindu, Christian, Buddhist	Taka (100 paisa)
Belgians	Belgium	French, Flemish, German	Christian	Belgian franc (100 centimes)
Belize, citizens of	Belize	English, American Indian languages	Christian, tribal religions	Belize dollar (100 cents)
Beninese	Benin	French, African languages: Fon, Adja, Bariba, Yoruba	Tribal religions, Christian, Muslim	Franc of the African financial community
Bhutanese	Bhutan	Dzongkha (a Tibetan dialect)	Buddhist, Hindu	Ngultrum (100 chetrum)

PEOPLE	WHERE THEY LIVE	LANGUAGE	RELIGION	CURRENCY
Bolivians	Bolivia	Spanish American Indian languages: Aymara, Quechua	Christian, tribal religions	Bolivian peso (100 centavos)
Botswanans	Botswana	Se-Tswana, English	Christian, tribal religions	South African rand
Brazilians	Brazil	Portuguese, American Indian languages	Christian, tribal religions	Cruzeiro (100 centavos)
British	United Kingdom	English, Welsh, Gaelic	Christian	Pound sterling (100 pence)
Bruneians	Brunei	Malay, Chinese, English	Muslim, Buddhist, Chinese religions	Bruneian dollar (100 cents)
Bulgarians	Bulgaria	Bulgarian, Turkish, Macedonian	Christian, Muslim	Lev (100 stotinki)
Burmese	Burma	Burmese, English	Buddhist, Muslim, Hindu, tribal religions	Kyat (100 pyas)
Burundi, citizens of	Burundi	French, African languages: Kiswahili, Kirundi	Christian and tribal religions	Burundi franc (100 centimes)
Cambodians: see Kampucheans				
Cameroonians	Cameroon	French, English, African languages	Tribal religions, Christian, Muslim	African financial community franc
Canadians	Canada	English, French	Christian	Canadian dollar (100 cents)
Cape Verdeans	Cape Verde Islands	Portuguese, Crioulo	Christian	Cape Verde escudo
Central African Empire, citizens of	Central African Empire	Sangho, French	Christian, tribal religions	African financial community franc
Chad, citizens of	Chad	French, Arabic, African languages	Muslim, Christian, tribal religions	African financial community franc
Chileans	Chile	Spanish	Christian	Chilean peso
Chinese	China, Taiwan, Hong Kong	Mandarin, other Chinese dialects, English	Buddhist, Chinese religions, Christian, Muslim	Yuan (100 fen), New Taiwan dollar, Hong Kong dollar
Colombians	Colombia	Spanish	Christian	Colombian peso
Comorians	Comoros	French, Comoran	Muslim, Christian	African financial community franc

PEOPLE	WHERE THEY LIVE	LANGUAGE	RELIGION	CURRENCY
Congolese	Congo	French, Bantu languages	Tribal religions, Christian	African financial community franc
Costa Ricans	Costa Rica	Spanish	Christian	Costa Rica colon
Cubans	Cuba	Spanish, English	Christian	Cuban peso
Cypriots	Cyprus	Greek, Turkish, English	Christian, Muslim	Cyprus pound
Czechoslovaks	Czechoslovakia	Czech, Slovak, Hungarian	Christian	Koruna (100 haleru)
Danes	Denmark	Danish	Christian	Danish Krone (100 øre)
Djiboutians	Djibouti	French, African languages	Muslim, Christian	Djibouti franc
Dominicans	Dominican Republic	Spanish	Christian	Dominican peso
Dutch	Netherlands	Dutch	Christian	Guilder (100 cents)
Egyptians	Egypt	Arabic	Muslim	Egyptian pound (100 piastres)
Ecuadoreans	Ecuador	Spanish	Christian	Sucre (100 centavos)
Equatorial Guineans,	Equatorial Guinea	Spanish, Fang, Bubi	Christian	Ekuele (100 centimos)
English	England	English	Christian	Pound sterling
Ethiopians	Ethiopia	Amharic, Galla, Somali	Muslim, Christian	Ethiopian dollar
Fijians	Fiji	English, Fijian, Hindi	Christian, Hindu	Fiji dollar (100 cents)
Filipinos	Philippines	Tagalog, English, local languages	Christian, Muslim, tribal religions	Filipino peso
Finns	Finland	Finnish, Swedish	Christian	Markka (100 pennia)
French	France	French	Christian	French franc (100 centimes)
Gabonese	Gabon	French and African languages: Fang, Eshira,	Christian, tribal religions	African financial community franc
Gambians	Gambia	English, African languages: Mandinka, Fula, Wollof	Muslim, Christian	Dalasi (100 butut)
Germans	East Germany, West Germany	German	Christian	East German mark (100 pfennige), Deutschmark (100 pfennige)
Ghanaians	Ghana	English, African languages	Christian, Muslim, tribal religions	New cedi (100 pesewas)
Gibraltar, people of	Gibraltar	English, Spanish	Christian	Gibraltar pound
Greeks	Greece	Greek	Christian	Drachma (100 leptae)

PEOPLE	WHERE THEY LIVE	LANGUAGE	RELIGION	CURRENCY
Grenadians	Grenada	English	Christian	East Caribbean dollar
Guatemalans	Guatemala	Spanish, American Indian languages	Christian	Quetzal (100 centavos)
Guineans	Guinea	French, African languages: Fulani, Susu, Malinke	Muslim, tribal religions	Syli (100 cauris)
Guinea-Bissauans	Guinea-Bissau	Portuguese, Creole, African languages: Balante, Fulani, Malinke	Tribal religions, Muslim	Guinean peso (100 centavos)
Guyanese	Guyana	English, Hindi, Urdu	Christian, Hindu	Guyanese dollar
Haitians	Haiti	Creole, French	Christian, Voodoo	Gourde (100 centimes)
Hondurans	Honduras	Spanish, American Indian languages	Christian	Lempira (100 centavos)
Hungarians	Hungary	Magyar	Christian, Jewish	Forint (100 filler)
Icelanders	Iceland	Icelandic	Christian	Icelandic Krona
Indians	India	Hindi and 15 other main languages	Hindu, Muslim, Christian, Sikh, Buddhist	Rupee (100 paisa)
Indonesians	Indonesia	Bahasa Indonesian, Javanese, Madurese, Sundanese	Muslim, Christian, Buddhist, Hindu	Rupiah (100 sen)
Iranians	Iran	Farsi	Muslim, Christian,	Iranian rial (100 dinars)
Iraqis	Iraq	Arabic, Kurdish,	Muslim, Christian	Iraqi dinar
Irish	Ireland	English, Gaelic	Christian	Irish pound (100 pence)
Israelis	Israel	Hebrew, Arabic, Yiddish	Jewish, Muslim	Israeli pound (100 agorot)
Italians	Italy	Italian	Christian	Italian lira
Ivory Coast, citizens of	Ivory Coast	African languages, French	Tribal religions, Muslim, Christian	African financial community franc
Jamaicans	Jamaica	English	Christian, Rastafarian	Jamaican dollar
Japanese	Japan	Japanese	Buddhist, Shinto	Yen (100 sen)
Jews	Israel and other countries	Hebrew, Yiddish or languages of countries where they live	Jewish	Money of countries where they live

PEOPLE	WHERE THEY LIVE	LANGUAGE	RELIGION	CURRENCY
Jordanians	Jordan	Arabic	Muslim, Christian	Jordanian dinar
Kampucheans	Kampuchea	Khmer, French	Buddhist	Riel (100 sen)
Kenyans	Kenya	English, African languages: Swahili, Kikuyu, Luo	Christian, tribal religions	Kenyan shilling (100 cents)
Koreans	North Korea, South Korea	Korean	Buddhist, Chinese religions, Christian	Won (100 jeon)
Kuwaitis	Kuwait	Arabic	Muslim, Christian	Kuwaiti dinar
Lao	Laos	Lao, French, English	Buddhist, tribal religions	Liberation kip (100 at)
Lebanese	Lebanon	Arabic, French,	Christian, Muslim	Lebanese pound (100 piastres)
Lesotho, citizens of	Lesotho	Sesotho, English	Christian	South African rand
Liberians	Liberia	English, African languages	Tribal religions	Liberian dollar (100 cents)
Libyans	Libya	Arabic	Muslim	Libyan dinar
Liechtenstein, citizens of	Liechtenstein	German	Christian	Swiss franc
Luxembourg, citizens of	Luxembourg	Letzeburgesch French, German	Christian	Luxembourg franc (100 centimes)
Malagasy	Malagasy Republic	Malagasy, French	Tribal religions, Christian, Muslim	Malagasy franc (100 centimes)
Malawians	Malawi	English, Nyanja	Tribal religions, Christian	Malawi kwacha (100 tambala)
Malaysians	Malaysia	Malay, English, Chinese, Indian languages	Muslim, Buddhist, Hindu, Christian	Ringgit (100 sen)
Maldivians	Maldives	Maldivian	Muslim	Maldivian rupee
Malians	Mali	Bambara, French	Muslim, tribal religions	Malian franc
Maltese	Malta	Maltese, English, Italian	Christian	Maltese pound (100 cents)
Mauritanians	Mauritania	French, Arabic	Muslim	Ouguiya (5 khoums)
Mauritians	Mauritius	English, Hindi, Creole, Urdu, French	Hindu, Christian, Muslim	Mauritian rupee (100 cents)
Mexicans	Mexico	Spanish	Christian	Mexican peso (100 centavos)
Monegasque	Monaco	French	Christian	French franc
Mongolians	Mongolia	Khalkha Mongolian, Russian	Buddhist	Tugrik (100 mongo)
Moroccans	Morocco	Arabic, Berber	Muslim, Christian	Dirham (100 centimes)

PEOPLE	WHERE THEY LIVE	LANGUAGE	RELIGION	CURRENCY
Mozambicans	Mozambique	Portuguese, African languages	Tribal religions, Christian, Muslim	Mozambican escudo (100 centavos)
Namibians	Namibia	Afrikaans, English, African languages	Christian, tribal religions	South African rand
Nauruans	Nauru	Nauruan, English	Christian	Australian dollar
Nepalese	Nepal	Nepali	Hindu, Buddhist, Muslim	Nepalese rupee (100 paisa)
New Zealanders	New Zealand	English, Maori	Christian	New Zealand dollar
Nicaraguans	Nicaragua	Spanish	Christian, tribal religions	Cordoba (100 centavos)
Niger, citizens of	Niger	French, African languages	Muslim, Christian, tribal religions	African financial community franc
Nigerians	Nigeria	English, African languages: Hausa, Ibo	Muslim, Christian, tribal religions	Naira (100 kobo)
Norwegians	Norway	Norwegian, Lapp	Christian	Norwegian krone (100 øre
Omanis	Oman	Arabic	Muslim	Omani rial
Pakistanis	Pakistan	Punjabi, Urdu, Sindhi, Pushtu	Muslim, Hindu, Christian	Pakistani rupee (100 paisa)
Panamanians	Panama	Spanish	Christian	Balboa (100 centesimos)
Papua New Guineans	Papua New Guinea	English, Pidgin, Moru	Christian, tribal religions	Kina (100 toea)
Paraguayans	Paraguay	Spanish, American Indian languages	Christian, tribal religions	Guarani (100 centimos)
Peruvians	Peru	Spanish, American Indian languages: Quechua, Aymara	Christian, tribal religions	Peruvian sol (100 centavos)
Poles	Poland	Polish	Christian	Zloty (100 groszy)
Portuguese	Portugal	Portuguese	Christian	Portuguese escudo (100 centavos)
Qatar, citizens of	Qatar	Arabic	Muslim	Qatar riyal (100 dirhams)
Romanians	Romania	Romanian, Magyar, German	Christian	Leu (100 bani)
Russians: see Soviet Union				
Rwandese	Rwanda	French, African languages: Kinyarwanda, Kiswahili	Christian, Muslim, tribal religions	Rwandese franc (100 centimes)
Salvadoreans	El Salvador	Spanish	Christian	Colon (100 centavos)
San Marino, citizens of	San Marino	Italian	Christian	Italian lira

PEOPLE	WHERE THEY LIVE	LANGUAGE	RELIGION	CURRENCY
São Tomé and Principe, citizens of	São Tomé and Principe	Portuguese	Christian	Conto
Saudi Arabians	Saudi Arabia	Arabic	Muslim	Saudi riyal (100 halalah)
Scots	Scotland	English, Gaelic	Christian	Pound sterling
Senegalese	Senegal	French, African language: Wolof	Muslim, Christian, tribal religions	African financial community franc
Seychellois	Seychelles	Creole, English, French	Christian	Seychellois rupee
Sierra Leoneans	Sierra Leone	English, African languages: Krio, Mende, Temne	Tribal religions, Muslim, Christian	Leone (100 cents)
Singaporeans	Singapore	Malay, Mandarin Chinese, Tamil, English	Muslim, Buddhist, Hindu	Singaporean dollar (100 cents)
Solomon Islanders	Solomon Islands	Roviana, Marovo	Tribal religions, Christian	Solomon Island dollar
Somalis	Somalia	Somali, Arabic, English, Italian	Muslim, Christian	Somali shilling (100 centesimi)
South Africans	South Africa	Afrikaans, English, African languages: Xhosa, Zulu, Tswana, Sesotho, Sepedi	Christian, Muslim, Hindu, tribal religions	South African rand (100 cents)
Soviet Union, citizens of	Union of Soviet Socialist Republics	Russian, Ukranian, Byelorussian, Latvian, Lithuanian, Estonian, Georgian, Armenian, Uzbek and others	Christian, Muslim, Jewish	Rouble (100 kopeks)
Spaniards	Spain	Spanish	Christian	Peseta (100 centimos)
Sri Lankans	Sri Lanka	Sinhala, Tamil, English	Buddhist, Hindu, Christian, Muslim	Sri Lankan rupee (100 cents)
Sudanese	Sudan	Arabic, Nilotic	Muslim, tribal religions	Sudanese pound
Surinamese	Surinam	Dutch, Hindustani, Javanese, Creole	Christian, Hindu, Muslim	Surinamese guilder (100 cents)
Swazis	Swaziland	English, African language: Siswati	Christian, tribal religions	South African rand
Swedes	Sweden	Swedish, Finnish, Lapp	Christian	Swedish krona (100 ore)
Swiss	Switzerland	German, French, Italian, Romanche	Christian	Swiss franc (100 centimes)
Syrians	Syria	Arabic	Muslim, Christian	Syrian pound (100 piastres)
Tanzanians	Tanzania	English, African language: Swahili	Christian, Muslim, tribal religions	Tanzanian shilling (100 cents)

PEOPLE	WHERE THEY LIVE	LANGUAGE	RELIGION	CURRENCY
Thais	Thailand	Thai	Buddhist, Muslim	Baht (100 satangs)
Togolese	Togo	French, African language: Ewe	Tribal religions, Muslim, Christian	African financial community franc
Tongans	Tonga	Tongan, English	Christian	Pa'anga (100 seniti)
Trinidad and Tobago, citizens of	Trinidad and Tobago	English, Hindi, French, Spanish	Christian, Hindu, Muslim	Trinidad and Tobago dollar (100 cents)
Tunisians	Tunisia	Arabic, French	Muslim, Jewish, Christian	Tunisian dinar
Turks	Turkey	Turkish, Kurdish	Muslim	Turkish lira (100 kurus)
Ugandans	Uganda	English, African languages: Luganda, Ateso, Runyankore	Christian, Muslim, tribal religions	Ugandan shilling (100 cents)
United Arab Emirates, citizens of	United Arab Emirates	Arabic	Muslim	United Arab Emirates dirham (100 fils)
Upper Voltans	Upper Volta	French, African language: Mossi	Tribal religions, Muslim, Christian	African financial community franc
Uruguayans	Uruguay	Spanish, American Indian languages	Christian, tribal religions	New Uruguayan peso (100 centesimos)
Vatican City, citizens of	Vatican City	Italian, Latin	Christian	Italian lira
Venezuelans	Venezuela	Spanish	Christian	Bolivar (100 centimos)
Vietnamese	Vietnam	Vietnamese	Buddhist, Chinese religions, Christian	Dong (100 xu)
Welsh	Wales	Welsh, English	Christian	Pound sterling
Western Samoans	Western Samoa	Samoan, English	Christian	Tala (100 sene)
Yemenites	North Yemen South Yemen	Arabic Arabic	Muslim Muslim	Yemeni riyal Yemeni dinar
Yugoslavs	Yugoslavia	Serbo-Croat, Slovenian, Macedonian	Christian, Muslim	Yugoslav dinar (100 para)
Zairians	Zaire	French, African languages: Lingala, Kiswahili, Tshiluba, Kikongo	Tribal religions, Christian	Zaire (100 makuta)
Zambians	Zambia	English, African languages: Nyanja, Bemba, Tonga, Lozi, Lunda, Luvale	Christian, tribal religions	Zambian kwacha (100 ngwee)
Zimbabweans	Zimbabwe	English, African languages: Sindebele, Shona	Christian, tribal religions	Rhodesian dollar (100 cents)

31

Sports and games

Board games

Chess has been played for over a thousand years and probably began in India. It is a game for two people, played on a black and white chequered board.

Backgammon is played a lot in Greece and the Middle East. It is probably one of the world's oldest games and is played by two people with dice and 30 pieces.

Mah jong is an ancient Chinese game which has been played for over 2,000 years. Four people play, with little "bricks" traditionally made of bone, or ivory and bamboo.

Go is a very old Japanese game. It is played by two people with round black and white pieces on a low table marked out with squares.

Cards are used all over the world to play many different games. They were probably invented in China about 1,50 years ago.

Fighting

Judo developed from the ancient Japanese method of fighting called *ju-jutsu*. It first became an Olympic Games sport in 1964.

Karate is another Japanese method of fighting. To avoid injury when it is played as a sport, punches, blows and kicks are pulled back before touching the opponent.

Boxing matches were held in the ancient Greek Olympic Games. The rules of the modern game were drawn up in 1867 by the Marquis of Queensberry of England.

Thai boxing is popular in Thailand and Japan. Opponents are allowed to punch, kick, knee and elbow each other and also to use leg throws.

Fencing is a sport which developed from sword fightin Opponents wear protective clothing and are not allowed to hit each other below the waist.

Football

Games in which stuffed leather balls were kicked around were played in China 2,000 years ago. **Soccer** is played by 2 teams of 11 players.

Rugby is played by 2 teams of 13 or 15 players. The ball is kicked or carried and points are scored by putting the ball over the goal line or kicking it over the crossbar.

In **American football**, players wear helmets and padding. Teams of 11 players tackle their opponents to stop them scoring by kicking goals or reaching the goal line.

Australian rules is played on an oval pitch by two teams of 18 players. Points are scored by kicking the ball between the opposite team's posts.

Gaelic football is played in Ireland by two teams of 15 players who try to score poin by putting the ball in or over their opponent's goal. Playe catch, fist and kick the ball.

Other ball games

Lacrosse is played in Europe and N. America and developed from a game played by North American Indians.

Hockey is played with curved sticks by teams of 11 players. In Canada, teams of five play hockey on ice.

Modern **cricket** developed in England and is played by two teams of 11 players which take turns to bat and score points with runs.

Golf, as it is played today, developed in Scotland. A small hard ball is hit with a stick called a club into small holes on the golf course. Usually played by two people.

Tennis developed from a French game called handball It is played by two or four players who hit a ball backwards and forwards ove a net with their rackets.

Basketball is an American game in which two teams of five players try to throw the ball into the opposite team's "basket". The ball may be bounced or thrown.

American **baseball** developed from the English game of rounders. Teams of 9 players hit the ball with a wooden bat and score points by running round the "bases".

Pelota is a Spanish game played in a three-walled court. Players hit the ball with a special wicker basket and score points if their opponent misses the ball.

The French game of **boules** is played by throwing metal balls so that they land near a small marker ball. Players score points for balls nearest to the marker.

Billiards, a game played on table with three balls which are hit with a stick, develope in England. Variations of the game are snooker and pool.

Houses round the world

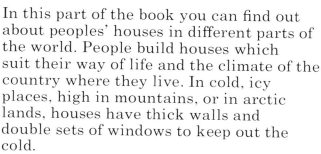

In this part of the book you can find out about peoples' houses in different parts of the world. People build houses which suit their way of life and the climate of the country where they live. In cold, icy places, high in mountains, or in arctic lands, houses have thick walls and double sets of windows to keep out the cold.

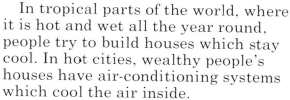

In tropical parts of the world, where it is hot and wet all the year round, people try to build houses which stay cool. In hot cities, wealthy people's houses have air-conditioning systems which cool the air inside.

People who live in deserts or dry grasslands and herd animals for a living need houses they can pack up and carry with them when they move to find new pastures. Herders in Mongolia live in round tents called yurts just like their ancestors did hundreds of years ago.

People build their houses with all sorts of different materials. Mud houses are cool to live in and mud is cheap and fairly easy to build with. Forest and jungle houses are often built with wood and thatched with leaves.

The pictures on this page show some of the houses you can read about in this part of the book.

Houses through the ages

1 About 350,000 years ago

In prehistoric times people hunted wild animals for food. They often followed the animals from place to place and camped a few days in huts built from branches and grass.

2 About 7,000 years ago

Later, when people learned how to plant crops and tame animals, they no longer needed to hunt. They settled down and built more solid houses. Some used mud baked hard by the sun.

3 About 3,500 years ago

Gradually the villages grew and became towns. In this crowded cit in ancient Egypt, people lived in houses four or five storeys tall, as they were short of building space. They paid specially trained

5 About 900 years ago

In the early Middle Ages, country people lived in cottages made of "wattle and daub". They made a wooden frame and then filled it in with woven sticks (the wattle) and mud paste (the daub).

6 About 900 years ago

The Normans, who came from France, used stone for building. Their houses had outside staircases. You can spot a Norman building by its rounded door and window arches.

7 About 600 years ago

Town houses in the Middle Ages were built very close together. The upstairs rooms overhung the street and almost touched. There were no drains and people threw their rubbish into the street.

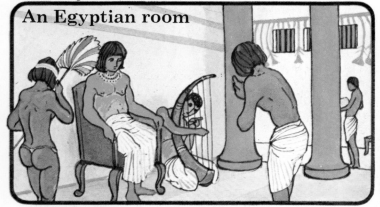

An Egyptian room

Egyptian houses, especially wealthy people's, were large and spacious. Small, high windows let in light and cool breezes, but kept out the glare of the hot summer sun. Guests were entertained in this hall.

Inside a peasant's cottage

Forests covered much of Europe in the Middle Ages, so wood was used for houses, furniture and even plates and bowls. Cottage floors were bare earth, trodden down hard and animals shared the living room. The fire mad the room smoky.

The Mbuti people live in the jungle in Zaire, Africa. They are Pygmies, a race of people who are only about 130cm tall. They live mainly by hunting and gathering.

At night they sleep in round huts made of branches and sticks covered with large jungle leaves. The leaves keep out the rain, but easily catch fire when dry, so the Mbuti light fires outside their houses. On cold nights they sleep outside beside the fire.

he Yanomamo people sleep in ammocks and store their few ossessions in the roof. Each anomamo family has its own rea under the roof. The roof is ade from the leaves of palm trees, id in layers over a framework of poles. Cool breezes blow in through a narrow gap between the roof and the ground. About every two years, when the roof starts to leak or is full of insects, the Yanomamo burn it down and build a new one.

Jungle houses in Peru

hese Amahuaca people f Peru are cutting back ne jungle to make a earing where they will ut up a new house.

They lash sticks together to build a wooden frame which they thatch with palm leaves.

This Amahuaca woman is making a pot from coils of clay. Women plant and harvest the crops and also prepare the food.

This is a small jungle town on the Amazon river. The houses are built on stilts or rafts to protect them from floods.

39

Tents and caravans

Wooden pins

Cheese made from goats' milk drying in the sun.

Redding

Churning milk in a goatskin to turn it to butter.

Pounding coffee beans to fine grains for making small cups of bitter black coffee.

Flour and water dough being made into flat loaves of bread.

Grinding wheat to make flour.

Some Bedouin keep a few hens for their eggs.

The Bedouin are Arabs who wander across the Arabian desert, herding camels, goats and sheep. They live in tents made of cloth woven from goat hair. Each tent has a dividing curtain.

On one side is the women's area where the family sleeps and the women cook. On the other side, the men receive their guests and hold meetings. When men from outside the family visit the tent, all the women hide. They hang another curtain from the tent rope so the men cannot see into their part of the tent.

Gypsy caravans

This gypsy family are camping beside the road in their horse-drawn caravan. Gypsies are descended from travelling people who came from India. Now they live all over Europe and the Middle East.

In this caravan there is an old-fashioned wood-burning stove for cooking. Cupboards and walls have traditional decorations.

Most gypsies now live in modern caravans. They camp by the roads or on special gypsy campsites.

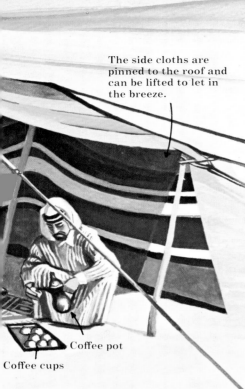

The side cloths are pinned to the roof and can be lifted to let in the breeze.

Coffee pot

Coffee cups

Inside the tent, the Bedouin sit on carpets. They have no furniture. When the guests arrive they bring out cushions for them to sit on.

How to make a tent

Here are some ideas for making tents indoors and outside.

WASHING LINE TENT
BLANKET
PEGS
STONES

CLOTHES-HORSE TENT
PEGS OR PINS
TWO BLANKETS

BACK OF SOFA TENT
BOOKS FOR WEIGHT
CUSHION
TORCH FOR LIGHT

TWO-CHAIR TENT
BLANKET
BOOKS
CUSHIONS TO SIT ON

✗ NEVER light a fire inside your tent.

These are some useful things for making tents: broomsticks, blankets, safety pins, books, cushions, stones.

1 Living in yurts

The Turcoman live in the desert in Iran, travelling from place to place in search of water and pastures. They live in tents called yurts, which they carry with them on their camels.

2

The Turcoman women pitch the yurts. They put up a wooden frame first, then cover it with pieces of felt. In winter they use several layers of felt to keep out the cold.

3

There are three areas inside the yurt: one for sleeping, one for the women and one for the men. The bedding is stored in the sleeping area at the back of the tent.

Clothes and cooking pots are hung on the women's side. Weaving equipment, bags of wheat and flour, saddles and guns are kept on the men's side.

4

Turcoman women make the felt for covering the yurts, and for carpets and saddle bags too. The felt is made from sheep's wool. The young girls comb out the wool. Then the women wet it and roll

and press it between reed mats until the wool becomes tangled and matted to form felt. They make carpets and bags with coloured patterns, but wall felts are white until fire smoke blackens them.

Ranches and farmhouses

Thatched farmhouse

Cowsheds
Dairy
Milk churns

This painted English farmhouse has changed very little since it was built about 300 years ago. It was made of local stone and thatched with straw. The farmer and his family still live in it. The cowsheds, barns for hay, animal feed and farm machinery surround the yard. Many farms are in the middle of their fields, away from other houses.

A Danish farmhouse

Old farmhouses in Denmark, like this one, were once the home of the farmer, his family and his animals. Now sheds and stables have been built for pigs, cattle, hay and machinery, round a yard at the back of the house. The animals are kept indoors from October to May when it is too cold for grazing. This farmhouse also has rooms for farm workers and summer guests.

Spanish farming village

Roof garden

Farmhouses in Spain are often built close together on the steep hillsides. This leaves the flat land in the valley clear for farming. On the ground floor are stables and a grape press for making wine. The farmer and his family live on the next floor. The top floor is used for store rooms.

A farm in Argentina

Store hut
Bread oven

In the countryside round the city of Cordoba, in Argentina, farmers have small houses built of mud bricks (sometimes called "adobe"). This farmhouse is surrounded by a fence to form a yard called a corral, where cattle, pigs and hens are kept at night. In the corral there is an oven, where the farmer's wife bakes her bread, and a well which provides drinking water. The farmer owns a small plot of land nearby where he grows vegetables and a few orange trees.

Farmers coming home from fields.

Grapevines

Drying sheep's wool

Drying vegetables

1 Life on a sheep station

Windmill

Sheep farms on the dry grasslands of Australia cover thousands of square kilometres. Farming families are often more than a day's drive from their nearest neighbours. Water has to be pumped up from underground streams by windmills. Supplies and letters come by plane.

Ranch-hands often ride motorbikes now, instead of horses, when they round up the sheep. They are helped by sheepdogs.

Children living on remote stations have lessons by two-way radio. They write their homework and post it to their teachers.

1 On a cattle ranch

the Rocky Mountains, in ontana, U.S.A., cattle ranches re huge. In winter, hay is taken y horse-drawn sledges to feed the attle. The cowboys live in wooden bunk houses near the ranch house. They now drive the cattle to market in large trucks, rather than herding them along the old cattle trails.

In spring the cowboys take the cattle up to the mountains looking for grass for grazing. They live in wooden cabins and cook over campfires.

43

Living on water

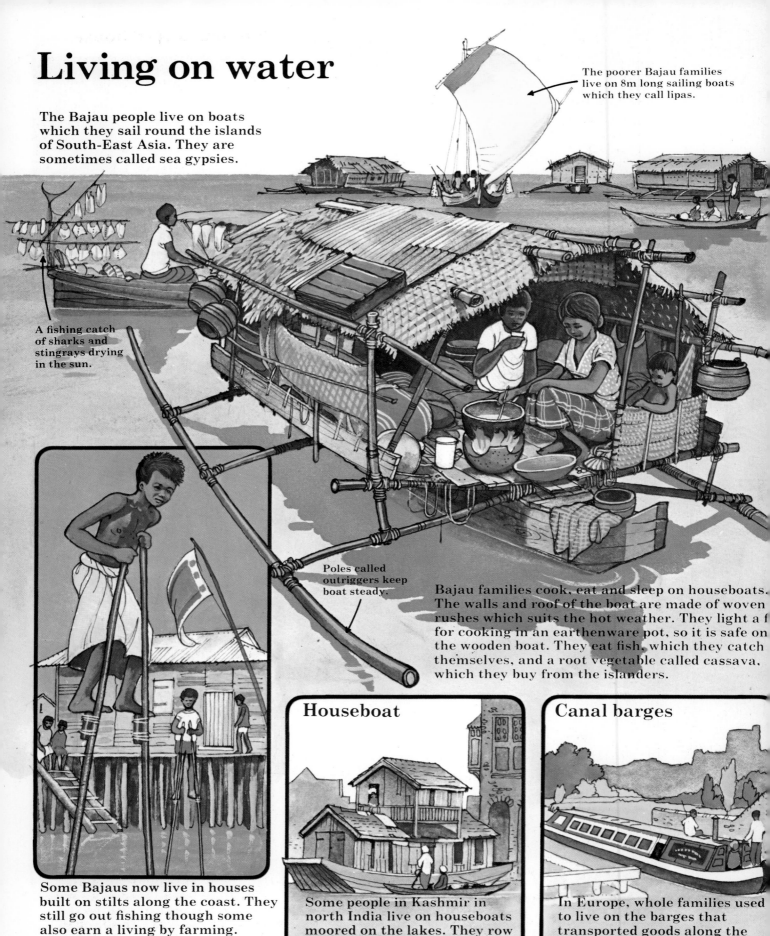

The Bajau people live on boats which they sail round the islands of South-East Asia. They are sometimes called sea gypsies.

The poorer Bajau families live on 8m long sailing boats which they call lipas.

A fishing catch of sharks and stingrays drying in the sun.

Poles called outriggers keep boat steady.

Bajau families cook, eat and sleep on houseboats. The walls and roof of the boat are made of woven rushes which suits the hot weather. They light a f for cooking in an earthenware pot, so it is safe on the wooden boat. They eat fish, which they catch themselves, and a root vegetable called cassava, which they buy from the islanders.

Some Bajaus now live in houses built on stilts along the coast. They still go out fishing though some also earn a living by farming. These children are using stilts to walk between the houses.

Houseboat

Some people in Kashmir in north India live on houseboats moored on the lakes. They row to land in small boats and do their shopping from shopboats.

Canal barges

In Europe, whole families used to live on the barges that transported goods along the canals. Today they are used mainly as holiday homes.

44

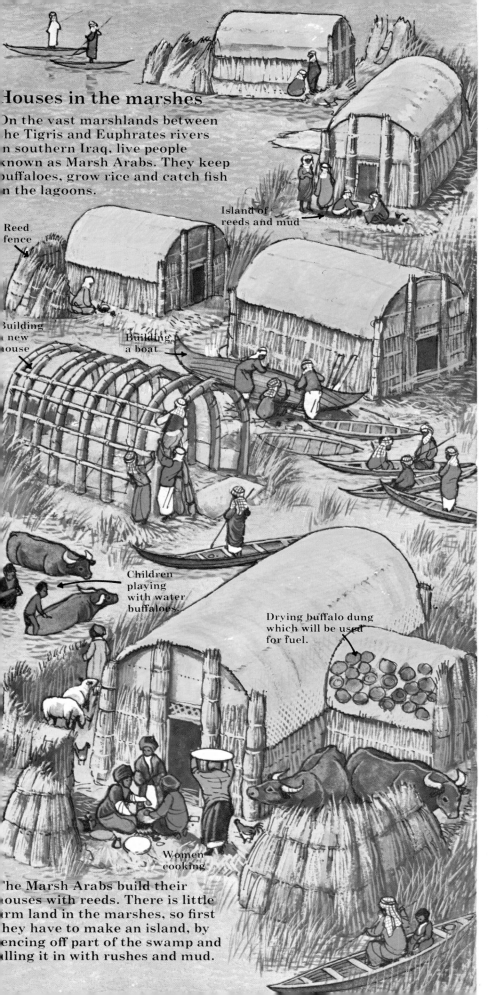

Houses in the marshes

On the vast marshlands between the Tigris and Euphrates rivers in southern Iraq, live people known as Marsh Arabs. They keep buffaloes, grow rice and catch fish in the lagoons.

Island of reeds and mud

Reed fence

Building a new house

Building a boat

Children playing with water buffaloes.

Drying buffalo dung which will be used for fuel.

Women cooking

The Marsh Arabs build their houses with reeds. There is little farm land in the marshes, so first they have to make an island, by fencing off part of the swamp and filling it in with rushes and mud.

Building a reed house

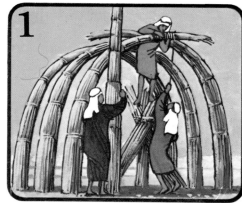

Bundles of giant reeds, cut from the marshes, are tied together and bent into a framework for the house. Ancient carvings show that this method of building was used here over 5,000 years ago.

Weaving wall mats

The walls and roofs of the Marsh Arabs' houses are made of mats woven from reeds. They sell spare mats in the local village markets. New wall mats have to be woven every few years as the reeds rot.

The houses are quite warm in winter as the matting keeps out the wind. Warmth from the fire dries out the reeds. In summer the walls are rolled up to let in the breeze.

45

Tree houses

In this look out, 12m up in the trees, men in India watched for enemies. Tree houses are not used as permanent homes, because it is very difficult to get water, food and firewood from the ground to the house. They are also easy for enemies to beseige or burn down.

Among some tribal peoples in New Guinea, young unmarried girls sometimes had to live in tree houses, and special ceremonies were held in them. Some even had fireplaces inside, made of clay or stone so they did not burn the house down.

Tree-stump house

The stump of this giant redwood tree has made a good solid platform for a house. It is used as a holiday house by its American owners.

Tree hide-out

This tree is big enough for four people to sit inside comfortably.

Baobab trees have extremely thick trunks. This one, which is in Africa, was hollowed out a long time ago as a hiding place during a war between two tribes. Since then, hunters have often sheltered in it and now it is a local landmark.

Building a tree house

If you want to build a treehouse, remember, it could damage the tree, so you should ask permission of the tree's owner first. If you live near an adventure playground, you could ask the playground leader if you could build a treehouse there. Never take candles or light a fire in a treehouse.

46

Living in caves

In 1971 a forest hunter called Dafal discovered some people called the Tasaday, living in caves in a remote valley in the Philippines. The entrances to their caves were high up in the rocks. To reach them they climbed trees or swung across on the long, rope-like stems of jungle plants.

When Dafal found them, the Tasaday were wearing clothes made from leaves, and using stone tools. They lived on wild plants and flowers, grubs, lizards, crabs and snakes.

1 Cave houses in Turkey

Pigeon houses

his strange landscape of cone-
aped rocks is in Turkey. The
ck is soft and easy to carve, and
r over 2,000 years local people
ve built their houses, churches
and monasteries in the rocks. They hollowed out the cones and put in wooden windows and doors. When the rock is exposed to the air, it hardens.

2

Inside their cave homes, the people cover the earth floors with carpets and paint the rocky walls. They have carved rock staircases which lead to more rooms upstairs.

French caves

These old caves in France have been made into modern homes by building on new fronts with windows and doors and adding chimneys.

High in the mountains

There are people living in even the highest mountain ranges of the world. It is cold and desolate there and they need sturdy, thick-walled houses to protect them.

Firewood is stored here on the roof.

These are prayer flags, hu on the roof to bring good luck.

Poorer families use oiled paper instead of glass in the windows.

This girl is spinning a prayer wheel as she recites prayers of the Buddhist religion.

This is the only doorway everyone has to go through the yak stable to get into the house.

These are the Lobas people, who live among the snow-capped peaks of the Himalayas in Nepal. The highest mountain in the world, Mount Everest, is not far away. There are no trees to shelter them from the wind, because it is too cold for them to grow.

This family's house is built of stone and mud-brick. The ground floor is used as a stable and heat from the animals' bodies helps keep the house warm. The people live upstairs. They farm a few crops and keep sheep, goats, and mountain animals called yaks.

Yaks carry heavy loads and pull ploughs. Their hair is used for clothing and their dung for fuel. The females called dris, supply milk, butter and cheese.

1 Mexican mountain farm

The Huichols are American Indians who live in the mountains of western Mexico. It gets bitterly cold in winter, though trees and cacti still grow there. They live in isolated family groups on farms called "ranchos", several hours' walk from each other. Here, the Huichols are holding a ceremony to wish the men good luck when they travel into the mountains.

Good luck crosses

Inside the house, the family has a wood-burning stove for cooking food. There is also a bamboo churn for brewing tea, which they drink with butter and salt.

Some families now have more modern equipment, such as thermos flasks and pressure cookers. They buy these on rare trading expeditions to the towns.

This is a demon trap. The Lobas hang these over their doorways to keep away evil spirits. Round the ram's skull is a picture of each person living in the house.

In summer, the Lobas leave their isolated houses and meet other families for parties and picnics. They camp in tents like this one.

Grinding maize

Gourd full of water

...e ranchos are groups of huts ...ade from stone and adobe (mud ...icks). The thatched roofs ...erhang the walls to protect them ...om heavy rain.

This hut is used for cooking. These Huichol are making "tortillas", thin flat pancakes made with maize, which they eat instead of bread or rice.

Good luck crosses

To make good luck crosses like the Huichols, you will need some straws and wool.

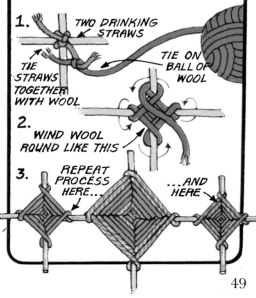

1. TWO DRINKING STRAWS
TIE STRAWS TOGETHER WITH WOOL.
TIE ON BALL OF WOOL

2. WIND WOOL ROUND LIKE THIS

3. REPEAT PROCESS HERE... ...AND HERE

Wooden houses and log cabins

1 Swiss chalets

In Switzerland, houses built of wood, like the farmhouse shown above, are called chalets. In the mountains and forested valleys, most of the houses are wooden.

In winter, the ground floor is used as a stable. This part of the house is built of stone so the damp does not rot it. The snow on the gently sloping roof helps to keep heat in.

Almost everything inside the chalet is made of wood, so there are strict laws about fire safety. The windows have double layers of glass to keep the house warm.

Old Japanese farmhouse

Inside the Japanese farmhouse, the family sleeps on a wooden platform covered with straw mat. In the past, there were no stables and the animals slept in here too.

Trays of silkworms

This is an old-fashioned farmhouse in Japan. It is built of wood and thatched with reeds. There is no glass in the windows. Instead they are covered with screens made of straw and sliding wooden shutters which keep out the snow. The two small buildings in front of the house are where animals are kept. This is called a Minka farmhouse.

The attics are mainly used for growing silkworms. At both ends there are windows to let in the sunlight.

Haystacks

Winter houses
in valley

Firewood

Cows wear
bells so their
owners can
find them.

summer, when the snow melts,
e villagers move higher up the
ountains to find good grass for
eir cows and to harvest hay
ady for the winter.

While they are there they live in
log cabins roofed with stones from
the mountain quarries. These are
much smaller and simpler than
their winter homes in the valleys.

They cut the long grass, stack it
and leave it to dry into hay. Before
the winter snows come they take
the hay and the animals back
down the mountain.

uilding wooden houses

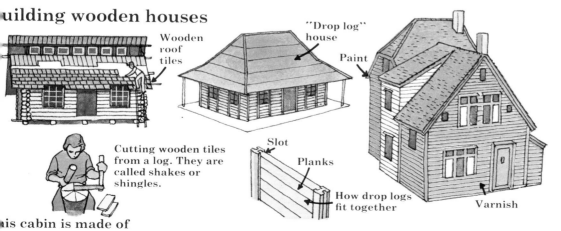

Wooden
roof
tiles

"Drop log"
house

Paint

Slot

Planks

Cutting wooden tiles
from a log. They are
called shakes or
shingles.

How drop logs
fit together

Varnish

is cabin is made of
gs which are fitted
gether at the corners
a criss-cross pattern.
is being roofed with
oden tiles.

In this house the planks
of wood are fitted into
slots in the upright
posts. These are called
"drop log" houses.

Wooden houses have to be
treated against insects
and painted or varnished
regularly, to prevent the
wood from rotting.

Some older wooden
houses are decorated
with carvings like this
one in eastern USSR.

Living in icy places

The coldest places on Earth are the arctic lands near the North Pole, and Antarctica, the land at the South Pole. The winters are very long and the summers are warm, but short. For most of the year the land and sea are covered with thick snow and ice. In winter, it is daylight for only a few hours each day, but in summer the days are very long.

The Lapps

The Lapps live in the arctic lands of Norway, Finland, Sweden and Russia. Their clothes are embroidered with different patterns depending on the area they come from.

In the past they lived by hunting and herding reindeer. Nowadays most Lapps live and work in small towns.

A few Lapp families still keep herds of reindeer. In spring, they leave their homes and travel with the animals to the coast to escape the heat and insects of summer. On the way, they live in tents which they carry with them on their sledges. Some Lapp herders now use snow-mobiles instead of sledges.

Inside a Lapp tent

Lapp herdsman lining his fur boots with dried grass to keep his feet warm.

Lapp tents are made from sticks covered with reindeer skins. The lay branches on the frozen ground inside the tent and cover them with fur rugs to keep out the cold

1 Living in frozen Antarctica

Ice breaker supply ship

The only people who live in Antarctica are scientists and explorers. All their food and supplies have to be taken to them by ship or plane.

During the long winter no ships or planes can reach Antarctica. It is so cold and windy that the scientists cannot go outside.

2

This "Sno-cat" is going to a research station which is in a tunnel 10m down in the ice.

3

In spring, when th first ship breaks through the ice, it brings letters and parcels from hom

They carry supplies of dried food which they cook over the fire in the tent. At night they wrap themselves in reindeer skins and lie down near the fire. Some Lapps now have modern canvas tents.

1 Eskimo houses

Teams of husky dogs pull sledges

Seal skin being cleaned

Eskimos used to live by hunting seals and whales. Now most of them work in towns and go hunting in their spare time for seal skins to sell. They live in Greenland, and in northern Canada, Alaska and Russia.

In these freezing lands, the Eskimos build their houses of wood and line them with fibreglass so that they stay warm inside. They build on rocks or oil drums sunk in the ice so the houses stay firm if the surface ice melts.

2

In the past, when Eskimos went hunting, they lived in igloos which they built with blocks of snow. Nowadays the hunters take tents with them or stay in huts.

3

It was quite warm inside the igloos. The icy walls were covered with fur rugs. Lamps burning whale oil gave off heat and light.

Eskimo hunter

This Eskimo hunter is hiding behind a white screen so the animals cannot see him against the snow. The hunters use rifles now instead of spears.

An Eskimo game

This game was good practice for spear-throwing. Eskimo children made little wooden spears and tried to thrust them through a ring made of bone.

1. GLASS
CARD
DRAW ROUND GLASS AND CUT CIRCLE OUT OF CARD

2. COIN
CARD CIRCLE
DRAW ROUND COIN AND CUT OUT CENTRE OF CARD CIRCLE

3. ROLL A SHEET OF NEWSPAPER TO MAKE A "SPEAR"

4.

PAPER SPEARS

Living together

Palm thatch roof

Bedding mats

Ladder carved from a log

A kibbutz

Children's house

Lessons outdoors

1 Chinese commune

These caves used to be houses, but are now pigsties.

A kibbutz is a village in Israel where everyone has a share in the land and property of the village. They work and eat together and meet to discuss kibbutz affairs. Sometimes children live in special houses, away from their parents.

Taichai village is part of a Chinese commune, where everyone works together on the land. They share the produce among themselves and with the other villages in the commune. Flat "terrace" have been cut into the hillsides to make farmlan

Washing clothes

Devil scares

Pounding rice

Underground houses

Mosque where people go to pray

Air vent

At Matmata, on the edge of the Sahara Desert, people build their houses below the ground. They dig about 9m down into the soft rock. Several other desert peoples also do this because there are not enough stones or trees with which to build houses. Under the ground they can find water and shelter from sandstorms. It is cooler there too during the hot days.

Tunnel entrance

Tunnel leading to surface

Store room

Well

Oven

In the dense jungle on the island of Borneo, people called the Dayaks live in longhouses like this one. Between 20 and 50 families live in one house, which they all help to build. There are separate rooms for each family along the outside and an open space, like a street, down the centre. The Dayaks live near rivers and they build their longhouses on stilts.

There is a central courtyard, open to the sky, which has doorways leading off into the underground rooms. Some of the rooms are for families to live in. Others are stables for their animals and storerooms where they keep grain to last them until the next harvest.

2

Fireplace

his is a store room, living room nd bedroom. The stone platform the family bed, which has a replace underneath to heat it in ld weather.

1 Tunnel homes

This is Coober Pedy, a small, hot, dusty town in southern Australia, where the average temperature in summer is 38°C. Most of the people are opal miners.

2

Some miners have made their homes in old mine tunnels. It is so much cooler there that tunnels · are now being dug specially for living in.

Villages

A village on stilts

School house

Well

splitting a coconut

This isolated village in Malaysia is called a kampong. It is built in a jungle clearing, where it is often very hot and wet. The houses are built on stilts to let the air blow round them and keep them cool and dry. There are no roads or shops and there is no electricity. All the water comes from a well in the middle of the village. There is a village school and also a shelter where the women gather to make baskets.

Village in West Africa

Every day of the week there is a market in one of the villages in the dry lands of West Africa, on the edge of the Sahara Desert.

Vegetable garden

Mud-brick house

Basket of millet

Towers for storing millet

The land is so dry in this part of Africa that the people find it difficult to grow enough to eat. Every few years they move to find more fertile land, and their old mud houses crumble and disappear from sight.

Beer made from millet

Chillis

Millet

Families live in groups of huts, built round yards and surrounded by walls. A village is made up of lots of scattered family groups, each with its farming land round it.

In the rainy season, the women grow ground nuts, chillies and vegetables in gardens near their houses. If they grow more than their families can eat, they sell it at one of the markets.

1 Island village

On the Greek island of Santorini the houses are built close together on the hillside above the harbour. The flat land on the island is kept for farming.

In summer it gets very hot and the houses are painted white to reflect the sunlight. Most houses have two storeys and an outside staircase.

After the baker has baked the bread in the morning, villagers who do not have ovens bring their midday meals to be cooked while his oven is still hot.

for
Nuts

1 An Indian village

When the women go to fetch water from the well, they also do their washing. Then they do not have to carry so much water home and can talk while they work.

England

In this Indian village the houses are made of stone and mud and are built around courtyards, where the women spend most of their time. The people here are Hindus. In the Hindu religion every family belongs to a special group called a "caste" which lives in a different section of the village.

In many English villages the houses face on to a green. There is usually a public house where people can meet, and a village church. People used to live and work in villages but now most of them travel to towns to work.

Cities

Cities round the world

1 Edinburgh, the capital of Scotland, grew up round a huge rock and castle where the people thought they would be safe from attack.

2 Eighty years ago Nairobi, in Kenya, was a village. When the railway was built, the city grew round it. Now giraffes in the Game Park can see modern blocks.

3 In the centre of New York are some of the highest skyscrapers in the world. The city began as a landing place for the first European settlers of America.

Living in cities

Some cities have grown over many centuries from villages or small towns. Others have grown up in just a few years. There is always a reason for a city to be where it is. People may have settled there because it was an easy place to defend from enemies, because it was a good centre for trade, or because it had the things needed for an industry.

1 In many cities, people live close together in old houses and flats. There are no gardens for children to play in.

2 On the edge of cities, richer people live in houses with gardens. They have to travel into the city centres to work.

3 There are not enough cheap houses in many cities. Poor people build shanty towns round them using wood, tin or mud.

4 So many people have moved into some cities, such as Calcutta in India, that there are no houses for them. They sleep in the streets.

5 Factories provide jobs for people but they may put smoke and dirt into the air. Travelling to them can be crowded and unpleasant.

6 Shop windows filled with radios, televisions and furniture bring visitors to cities. Some may stay, hoping to find work.

7 In cities there are hospitals and doctors. People come in from the countryside where there may be no doctors to care for them.

Sydney, on the coast of Australia, was founded where inlets made a natural, safe harbour. This is now crossed by ferries and a huge bridge.

Cairo stands on the River Nile in Egypt, near the ancient pyramids of Giza. It is Africa's most crowded city. Every day more people come, looking for jobs.

Rio de Janeiro lies beneath Sugar Loaf Mountain on the coast of Brazil. It has fine houses on the beaches but shanty towns have been put up on the hillsides nearby.

New York street

During the hot summers in New York and other cities, many people sit, talk and play in the streets. It is cooler there than in their small flats and houses. The streets are closed to traffic on some special holidays and parties are held on the pavements and in the roads.

Parks in cities are pleasant places for people to walk and for children to play. The trees give shade for people to sit in and help to improve the air in smoky cities.

Adventure playgrounds have been built in some city centres, often on unused land. Here children can play and have fun, safe from the traffic on the roads.

Sports centres, stadiums and swimming pools are built in cities. Here, large numbers of people can watch and learn many sports.

Special places to live

Living on an oil rig

1 Fresh water and food have to be taken to the rig by boat. In rough seas, only helicopters can reach the rig.

2 Even in their cabins, the men can hear the constant noise of the drill. Every room has an alarm bell, in case of fire.

Alarm bell

3 Workers on the drilling platform are called roughnecks. There is always someone working as the drill never stops.

Oil rigs are built on shore and towed out to sea. The legs are filled with water to make them sink.

Tanks filled with water.

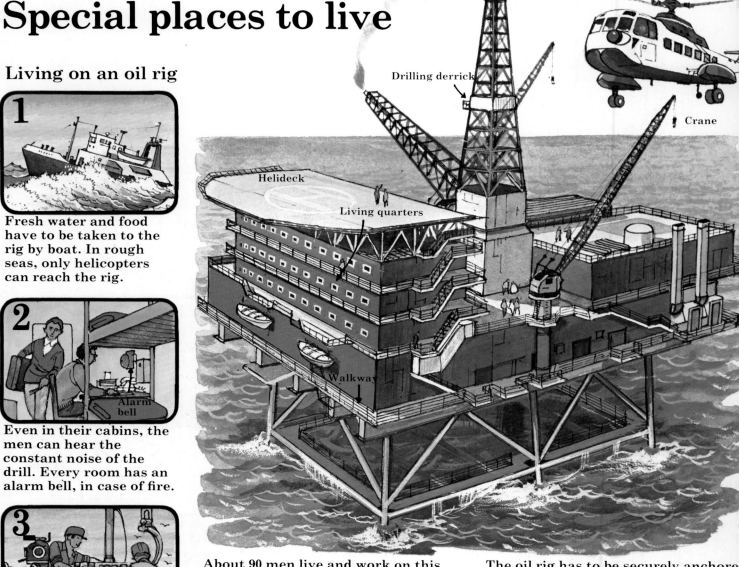
Drilling derrick

Crane

Helideck

Living quarters

Walkway

About 90 men live and work on this oil rig. They spend seven days on the rig, working 12 hour shifts and then fly ashore by helicopter for a week's leave.

The oil rig has to be securely anchored to the sea bed so that it does not break loose in rough seas. Divers regularly check the massive anchors which hold it in place.

Dome house
Domes, like this, have been built by people experimenting with new kinds of houses. They even used old car bodies.

Zome house
1 This "Zome" house is heated by the sun. The walls are made of a special material which keeps heat in.

2 Drums filled with water

One wall of the zome is lined with drums filled with water. The sun heats the water and the hot water heats the house.

Lighthouse

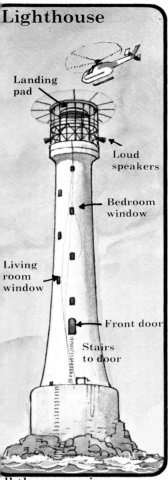

Landing pad

Loud speakers

Bedroom window

Living room window

Front door

Stairs to door

[A]ll the rooms in a [li]ghthouse are round and [th]e beds are curved to [fi]t the walls. These have [to] be very thick to [wi]thstand the pounding [o]f the waves. Three men [li]ve here, looking after [th]e light and foghorn. [H]elicopters land on the [la]nding pad on the top [ev]en in rough weather.

Under the sea

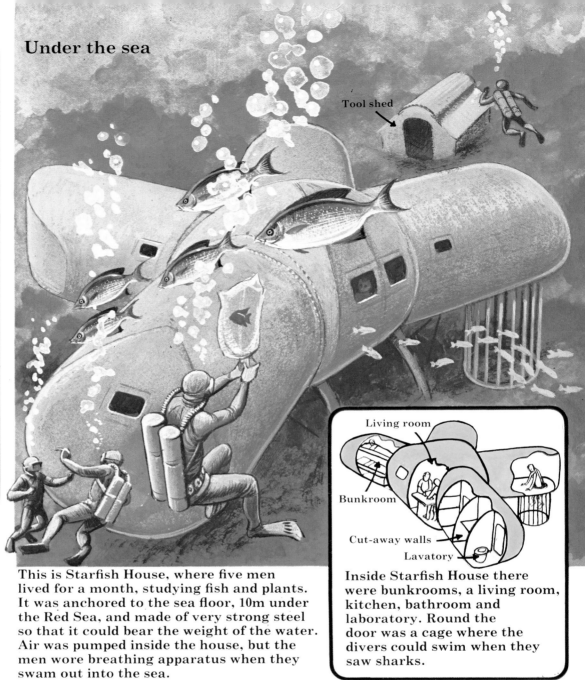

Tool shed

This is Starfish House, where five men lived for a month, studying fish and plants. It was anchored to the sea floor, 10m under the Red Sea, and made of very strong steel so that it could bear the weight of the water. Air was pumped inside the house, but the men wore breathing apparatus when they swam out into the sea.

Living room

Bunkroom

Cut-away walls

Lavatory

Inside Starfish House there were bunkrooms, a living room, kitchen, bathroom and laboratory. Round the door was a cage where the divers could swim when they saw sharks.

Space city

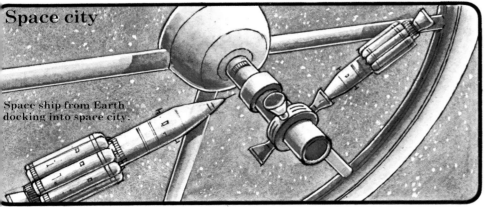

Space ship from Earth docking into space city.

[I]n the future, people may live in [c]ities in space, rather than on the [c]rowded Earth. This vast space [ci]ty would spin round so that [it] would feel like being on Earth.

Giant mirrors would reflect sunlight into the city and energy from the sun would be used for power and heat. Special screens would protect it from harmful rays.

Inside space city

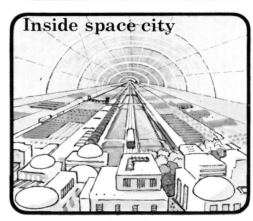

Inside the spokes of space city there would be houses, factories and farmland. There would be air inside the city so people could breathe normally.

Building materials

Stone

Stone makes strong, fire-proof, long-lasting buildings, though it is heavy to lift and transport. Mortar, a mixture of sand, cement* and water, is usually used to hold the stones together. Stones stacked up without mortar make "dry" stone walls.

Quarry where stone is cut from the ground.

House built of roughly cut stones held together with mortar.

"Dry" stone domed roofs on houses in southern Italy.

Concrete

Concrete is a modern building material made of gravel (tiny stones), sand and cement. Mixed with water, it makes a stiff paste which sets hard in hours. When steel rods are added, it is called reinforced concrete and is extremely strong.

Concrete, brought ready-mixed in a tanker, is piped into moulds.

Ready-made concrete walls are lifted into place by giant cranes.

Bricks

When clay is baked at high temperatures, it becomes very hard. It is used for making building bricks, roof tiles and pipes. Different coloured bricks are made from clays found in different places.

Brick factory where clay is moulded and baked into bricks.

Bricklayers always use mortar to hold bricks in place.

Mud

Mud is plentiful, cheap and easy to work with. It is often mixed with chopped straw to give it extra strength. Some soils bake rock-hard in the sun and may last for hundreds of years, though mud houses need regular repairs.

Mud paste is pressed into wooden moulds and left to dry into bricks.

Dry earth is rammed into hard bricks in this machine.

Houses made of mud bricks held together with mud paste.

Wood

Wood rots easily in damp weather and must be given regular coats of paint or varnish to protect it. It also catches fire easily. In forested places, it is a cheap building material. It is widely used for making roof frames.

Tree trunks are cut into planks at saw mills.

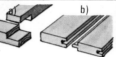
Two ways of joining wood: a) a corner joint, b) planks side-by-side.

House built with smoothed planks of wood in southern U.S.A.

Small house in Canada built of whole logs, joined with nails.

Bamboo, grass and leaves

Bamboo plants grow quickly in hot, wet countries and their stems make a strong and flexible, but very light, building material. Grass, reeds and leaves are light and waterproof too, though when dry they easily catch fire.

House walls made of bamboo poles split lengthways and woven.

African house woven like a giant basket from split bamboo.

House made of tall reeds by Marsh Arab people in Iraq.

Lakeside house in Peru made of reeds sewn into mats.

Wool and skins

People who move around with their herds of animals need light, portable homes. They often make them from animal skins or hair, supported by branches or wooden poles. Unwashed wool contains natural oils which make it waterproof.

Turcoman woman from Iran making tent felt from sheep's wool. The wool is beaten with sticks and rolled so its fibres tangle together into thick felt.

The pieces of felt are stretched over a wooden frame to make a large tent called a yurt. Smoke turns the white felts black after a few years.

Building to suit the climate

Here are some of the ways people make their houses suit the climate they live in.

Thick walls keep the heat out in summer and the cold out in winter.

Houses with windows facing a courtyard keep cool and shady.

Pale colours reflect the sun's rays so walls do not absorb their heat.

Shutters made of slats of wood (louvres) let in cool breezes, but keep out the sun's glare.

Wooden shutters protect windows from strong winds and snow-storms.

Windscoops direct wind down into houses in this hot Pakistani town.

*Cement is made from a rock called limestone. It sets very hard when mixed with water.

made of stone
d slate, which can
lit into thin sheets.

Grand city house built
of smoothed and
neatened stone blocks
and mortar.

Paint on walls helps
stop stones being worn
away by weather.

House walls made of
pebbles or pieces of
flint set in mortar.

Softer kinds of stone, ▶
such as sandstone, can
be carved. Only special
buildings, like palaces
and castles, usually
have carvings.

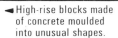
◀ High-rise blocks made
of concrete moulded
into unusual shapes.

Reinforced concrete is ▶
so strong, it can be used
to make overhanging
roofs and balconies.

Concrete is usually a ▶
dull grey colour, but it
can be coloured to make
towns more attractive.

made of clay tiles.
overlap to keep
e rain.

These tiles are a
different shape—like
pipes cut in half.

Roman brick building.
Their bricks were
smaller than modern ones.

Bricks were used a lot
for building about 100
years ago.

Decorated chimneys
made by skilled
bricklayers.

Patterned house wall
made by using different
coloured bricks.

built by pouring
into a wooden
e.

Four-storey mud brick
houses in Saudi Arabia.

"Cob" house in England.
Walls are built of layers
of mud paste and straw.

Houses built by the
Masai people of east
Africa from cow dung.

Houses in Morocco built
with mud bricks made in
patterned moulds.

Mud house in Nigeria
which has been painted.

apping planks,
d weather-boards,
this house.

Timber frame house,
with walls filled in
with bricks.

Frame for jungle house
made with naturally
forked branches.

House in Burma built
by weaving thin strips
of wood together.

Roof of wooden tiles,
called "shingles". It is
steep so rain runs off.

Carved wood is often
used to decorate houses,
even brick or stone ones.

grass house made
ving mats over a
e of branches.

House in Ethiopia being
covered with waterproof
bamboo leaves.

Palm leaves being
knotted together ready
for making a roof.

House with finished
palm leaf roof, called
palm thatch.

Roof being thatched
with bundles of straw
or reeds.

House in Europe with
straw thatch. It is
steep so rain runs off.

uin women weave
strips of cloth for
tents from a

mixture of sheep's wool
and goat hair.

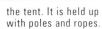
The woven strips are
sewn together to make
the walls and roof of

the tent. It is held up
with poles and ropes.

The Lapps use reindeer ▶
skins to make their
tents. The skins are
stitched together and
stretched over a hollow
cone of branches tied
together at the top.

◀ In some hot countries,
wire mesh is put over
windows to keep out
insects.

▼ Flat roofs are common
in hot, dry places. They
make a cool place for
sleeping at night.

▼ Thick rounded roofs on
houses in Greece keep
out summer heat.

▲
Gently sloping roofs
hold a blanket of snow
which keeps house
warm.

◀ In places where it rains
a lot, roofs are often
steep so it runs off.

Jutting-out roofs protect ▶
walls from rain and
provide shelter.

In hot, wet places,
stilts protect houses
from flooding and allow
cooling breezes to blow
under them.

House words

Here are some words to do with houses and what they mean. Look out for different kinds of roofs, windows and other parts of houses when you are walking or driving around.

Each floor of a building is called a **storey**. One-storey houses, like this one, are sometimes called bungalows.

Tall blocks of flats with several storeys are called **multi-storey** buildings.

This house is **detached**, which means that it is not joined on to any other houses.

A **semi-detached** house is joined to another house on one side only.

Houses joined to other houses on both sides a called **terraced** houses

Parts of a house

The underneath parts of a roof where it overhangs a wall are called the **eaves**.

A **lintel** is a long piece of stone or wood over a window or door to hold up the wall above.

A strip of plaster or wood between a wall and roof is a **cornice**.

Decorated boards along the edge of a roof are called **bargeboards**.

A room with glass walls and roof, built on to the side of a house is a **conservatory**.

A **balcony** is a platfor built on the outside of an upper floor of a building.

A triangular-shaped end wall of a building is called a **gable end**.

The beams which support an overhanging upper floor make a **jetty**.

Large stones which strengthen and protect the corners of buildings are called **cornerstones**.

A round or triangular-shaped decoration over a window is called a **pediment**.

A platform with a roof but no wall, round the outside of a house is a **verandah**.

A **patio** is a paved are or courtyard outside a house.

Roofs

A roof with slopes on all sides is called a **hipped roof**.

A roof with two slopes on each side, the lower one steeper than the upper, is a **mansard roof**.

A **castellated roof** ha battlements to make it look like an old castle

This curly shape at the edge of a roof is called a **Dutch gable**.

A roof with slopes on all sides, with some slopes shorter than others, is a **half-hipped roof**.

A roof which slopes on two opposite sides only is called a **gabled roof**.

The step shapes at the end of this gabled roof are called **crow-steps** or **corbie-steps**.

Many modern buildings have **flat roofs** of reinforced concrete.

Two gabled roofs side by-side on a building make an "M"-shape gable.

Windows and doors

Windows that open outwards on hinges are **casement windows**.

A three-sided window in a wall jutting out from a building is a **bay window**.

A **dormer window** is a small window sticking out from a sloping roof.

A tall arched window with a shorter, flat-topped window on each side is a **Venetian window**.

Windows, like these, made of strips of glass are called **louvred windows**.

A door which opens in two halves, like this, is called a **stable door**.

Windows with frames that slide up and down are called **sash windows**.

A window which juts out from an upper floor is an **oriel window**.

Long windows which reach to the floor and are used as doors are called **French windows**.

A **lattice window** is made of small diamond-shaped pieces of glass, with lead between them.

A semi-circular or fan-shaped window over a door is called a **fanlight**.

A flat window in a roo is called a **skylight**.

64

Index